ADVANCE PRAISE

"This is a book born in the barricades, neighborhood assemblies, and factory occupations of Argentina's 2001 uprising against neoliberalism. Written by movement participants, it's an inspiring account of the rebellion and a grassroots model of how to research and theorize a movement that forged a new way of doing politics from below. The English translation of such a classic book that's been passed around revolutionary circles for decades is a cause for celebration and hitting the streets!"—**Benjamin Dangl**, author of *The Five Hundred Year Rebellion: Indigenous Movements and the Decolonization of History in Bolivia*

"Twenty years ago, Argentina erupted in blockades and assemblies, occupations, demonstrations, and communal kitchens. In both its circumstances and forms, the 2001 uprising presaged the protests of 2011 and the struggles of our time. Colectivo Situaciones' *19 & 20* provided both the sharpest analysis of that moment and a model of theoretical practice: nimble, dialogical, embedded in the movements with whom it thought, made it common. To rediscover it today is to do more than reconnect with the recent past; it is inevitably also to ask how it illuminates what we have lived since, and how we can continue to extend its lessons into the future."—**Rodrigo Nunes**, author of *Neither Vertical Nor Horizontal: A Theory of Political Organization*

"A long decade before Occupy Wall Street, Argentineans poured into the streets to reject austerity and short the circuits of neoliberal capitalism, proving that state violence was no match for popular refusal. But this is not a book about Argentina or even Latin America as a whole, a brutal laboratory where neoliberalism was imposed in blood and fire. It's about a way of thinking that is also a doing, about what the concrete experience of rebellion teaches us about how the world moves, and how to turn that movement into thought. Find yourself in this book."—**Geo Maher**, author of *Building the Commune* and *A World Without Police*

"The 2001 uprising in Argentina is a major flashpoint in a wave of popular struggles that repudiated the neoliberal capitalist order and authored new forms of noncapitalist social construction. Colectivo Situaciones gives us important analyses of the uprising and its legacies, the roots of Argentina's financial and political crisis, and changes in contemporary forms of anticapitalist mobilization and resistance. Their close attention to grassroots practices of resistance, political organizing, and world-making is emblematic of their method of militant research, which itself has been an inspiration to so many. Those interested in contemporary social movements, political theory, and the history of Argentina and the region will find much to appreciate in this wonderful new edition."—**Jennifer S. Ponce de León,** author of *Another Aesthetics Is Possible: Arts of Rebellion in the Fourth World War*

"If the insurrection in Argentina that began in December 2001 was our Paris Commune, then Colectivo Situaciones fits well in the position of Karl Marx. As Friedrich Engels was fond of saying, one of Marx's many talents was to analyze the historical importance of political events as they took place. This book by Colectivo Situaciones, written in the heat of action, certainly demonstrates that same talent in full, delving into the complexity of concrete events while simultaneously stepping back to recognize how our political reality has changed."—**Michael Hardt**, author of *The Subversive Seventies* and coauthor of *Assembly*

GENOCIDE
IN THE
NEIGHBORHOOD

Philadelphia, PA
Brooklyn, NY
commonnotions.org

Genocide in the Neighborhood: State Violence, Popular Justice, and the 'Escrache'
Colectivo Situaciones
Translated by Brian Whitener, Daniel Borzutzky, and
Fernando Fuentes

Originally published as *Genocida en el Barrio: Mesa de Escrache
Popular* by Colectivo Situaciones (Tinta Limón, 2002). English
language edition first published by ChainLinks (Oakland and
Philadelphia), by series editors Jena Osman and Juliana Spahr.

ISBN: 978-1-942173-86-1 (print)
ISBN: 978-1-945335-02-0 (eBook)
LCCN: 2023949491

10 9 8 7 6 5 4 3 2 1

Common Notions
c/o Interference Archive
314 7th Street
Brooklyn, NY 11215
www.commonnotions.org
info@commonnotions.org

Common Notions
c/o Making Worlds
210 South 45th Street
Philadelphia, PA 19104

Discounted bulk quantities of our books are available for organizing, educational, or fundraising purposes. Please contact
Common Notions at the address above for more information.

Cover design by Josh MacPhee
Layout design by Morgan Buck and Margaret Killjoy
Typesetting by Suba Murugan

GENOCIDE IN THE NEIGHBORHOOD

State Violence, Popular Justice, and the 'Escrache'

By

COLECTIVO SITUACIONES

Translated by

BRIAN WHITENER, DANIEL BORZUTZKY, AND FERNANDO FUENTES

With an Introduction by

BRIAN WHITENER

CONTENTS

Preface   ix

Introduction
  Brian Whitener   1

The Escraches of HIJOS: Reasons and
  Motives   25

The Escraches: 9 Hypotheses for Discussion   29

Colectivo Situaciones in Conversation
  with HIJOS   37

A Text for the Escrache of Weber
  (a document of HIJOS)   69

12 Hypotheses / Questions Concerning
  the Escraches   75

Colectivo Situaciones in Conversation
  with the Mesa de Escrache Popular   87

If There Is No Justice, There is Escrache:
  Concerning the Discussion with the
  Mesa de Escrache Popular   133

Contributors   139

PREFACE

The book you hold in your hands should be known by every abolitionist and the *escrache* should be a part of every conversation about nonstate forms of justice. *Genocide in the Neighborhood* is a manual, a study, and a dialog about how to produce justice under conditions of impunity, when the state's rotten forms of false justice have failed.

From 1976 to 1983, Argentines suffered under the rule of a military dictatorship which came to power amidst the twin crises of economic downturn and rising working-class power. To restore accumulation and ruling-class control, the dictatorship, as a part of the CIA-backed Operation Condor, killed and/or disappeared an estimated 30,000 militants. The strategy repurposed pieces of a carceral framework (such as clandestine detention centers) with two apparatuses less often used in the US-context: forced disappearance and extermination.

For decades, brave groups like the Madres and Abuelas de la Plaza de Mayo risked imprisonment, censure, and violence to demand the return of their missing loved ones. *Aparición con vida* (or "Appearance with life") was the (often impossible) demand these groups organized around.

The dictatorship ended and the terribly misnamed process of redemocratization began. However, instead of members of the dictatorship being brought to justice, they were given legal immunity, sweeping their violence, and the deaths and disappearances, under the rug. At the end of the 1990s, the group HIJOS (Hijos por la Identidad y la Justicia contra el Olvido y el Silencio, Children for Identity and Justice against Forgetting and Silence), made up primarily of children whose parents had been disappeared by the dictatorship, began organizing against this state of impunity using a technique called the "escrache."

As I wrote in the original introduction to this book, "like all truly innovative practices, what an escrache *is* is rather difficult to define: it's something between a march, an action or happening, and a public shaming." Part carnival, part wake, part direct action. For a taste, search YouTube for Marcelo Expósito's video "Escrache a Videla."[1] For each escrache, HIJOS would select a member of the dictatorship, someone with a documented past of direct involvement in forced disappearance and extermination. Months of organizing in the genocidist's neighborhood followed. Members of HIJOS would knock on doors, hold meetings, hand out flyers to inform the other residents that there was a genocidist in their midst. After this consciousness raising work, a date for the escrache would be set, and on this day, HIJOS, other groups, and neighbors would assemble in front of the genocidist's place of residence for speeches, performances, and, at the very end, a marking of the house with paint or some other material.

The slogan of the escraches was "si no hay justicia, hay escrache" or "if there is no justice, there is escrache." The point of the escrache was to produce a situation of "social

---

[1] Escrache a Videla organized by HIJOS Buenos Aires, https://www.youtube.com/watch?v=XGFOZWRxK1g

condemnation." As one member of HIJOS puts it in this book, the aim was "to turn the neighborhood into a prison . . . tomorrow the shop owner won't sell to him; the taxi-driver won't pick him up; the baker will choose not to wait on him; the paperboy will refuse to deliver the newspaper."

The escrache then is a practice of transformational justice (and I use the present tense as the escrache has recently been given new life by feminist groups across Latin America organizing against patriarchal violence). It is a partial, provisional answer to the question of how to produce another justice, an alternative one, in conditions of impunity and institutional failure. The questions and problematics that the escrache confronts are the same that abolitionists worldwide are now grappling with.

Neither HIJOS, nor their interlocutors, Collective Situaciones, are dogmatists. So in this book, you will find more questions than answers, but there is also a horizon of a different justice. Let us, as the Zapatistas say, *caminar preguntando* (walk while asking questions) toward it together.

INTRODUCTION

brian whitener

1

THE TRANSLATORS FIRST conceived of this project because *Genocide in the Neighborhood* was a book that affected us, a book that, after the collapse and fragmentation of the antiglobalization movement, restored our faith in the possibilities of radical political practice, the necessity of experimentation, and the role of affect in constructing new forms of collectivity outside of the party. It is our hope that this book and its discussion of a particular radical autonomist political practice will find some resonance in a post-crisis United States and serve as a spur to further political creativity.

With this translation we want to provide an introduction to two groups and one practice, all of which emerged during the radicalization of Argentina in the late 1990s: the militant research group Colectivo Situaciones, the international human rights organization HIJOS (Hijos por la Identidad y la Justicia contra el Olvido y el Silencio, Children for Identity and Justice against Forgetting and

Silence), and the practice created by HIJOS in collaboration with other Argentine groups, the escraches.

2

COLECTIVO SITUACIONES IS a militant research collective based in Buenos Aires, Argentina. Militant research means that Situaciones works with other collectives and radical groups, both in Argentina and elsewhere in Latin America, to collaboratively produce new types of knowledge about current political practices and the social and political environments in which those practices take place.[1] I should note that "militant" doesn't mean military; however, we will use this translation throughout the text, because the common translation for the Spanish word *militante*—"activist"—is too weak of a term. Militant signifies a stronger commitment to political struggle (and not just community work) and a stronger commitment to a politicized collectivity.[2]

---

[1] The roots of militant research can be traced back to the questionnaire Marx wrote for workers in the *Revue Socialiste* in 1880, but more recent forms of militant investigation would include feminist consciousness raising groups and action research. The term militant research applies to any research practice that attempts to overcome the hierarchy between theory and practice, the investigator and the investigated, the political and the personal. All types of militant research practice attempt to create and test new methods for the production of collective knowledge, rather than simply replicate established forms of knowledge production. In the present moment of cognitive capitalism wherein knowledge production has been almost entirely subsumed under capital, militant research has become increasingly important. For those interested in more information, a good place to start is the "Militant Investigation" volume of the webjournal *transversal* (transform.eipcp. net/transversal/0406).

[2] For an absolutely brilliant discussion of the difficulties in translating this term and the stakes for the practice of Colectivo Situacio-

Situaciones was formed in the late 1990s as part of a massive response to the wide-spread layoffs and shredding of the social fabric that resulted from the neoliberalization of the Argentinian economy. Before the economic and social crisis crested with the toppling of the government of De la Rúa after the "popular insurrection" of December 19 and 20, 2001, scores of new movements were born, from assemblies barriales (neighborhood organizations) and fabricas recuparadas (factories taken over by their workers) to new organizations like Movimiento de Trabajadores Desocupados (Movement of Un-Occupied Workers) and HIJOS. These were movements which, for the most part, existed outside of the traditional left party organizations and whose politics and practices were heavily autonomist, meaning they sought politics outside of traditional party politics and the traditional left goal of seizing state power.[3]

As stated above, Colectivo Situaciones' ongoing intervention (which has played an important role in the resurgence and reframing of contemporary ideas of the left, politics, and militancy in Argentina, as well as the world over via numerous internet translations and conversations) concerns the production of knowledge using militant research. Situaciones developed their particular style of militant research as a way of working with the new movements that

---

nes please see Nate Holdren and Sebastian Touza, "Introduction to Colectivo Situaciones" in the journal *ephemera* (5.4: 595-601), as well as their pioneering translation of Situaciones in the same issue (www.ephemeraweb.org).

[3] The resources on these groups available in English are limited, but for more information see Lavaca Collective *Sin Patrón: Stories from Argentina's Worker-Run Factories* (Haymarket, 2007); Marina Sitrin (ed.) *Horizontalism: Voices of Popular Power in Argentina* (AK Press, 2006); and Stevphen Shukaitis (ed.) and David Graeber (ed.) *Constituent Imagination: Militant Investigation // Collective Theorization* (AK Press, 2007).

were rapidly proliferating on the Argentinean scene. Their goal was, and is, not to treat them as "objects" of study, but rather to find ways of expanding and furthering these movements' practices via collaborative investigation and to search for points of contact—points of contact which occur outside of party politics—between individual movements. Militant research, as practiced by Situaciones, is a method in the best of Marxist traditions in that it concerns itself with both theory and practice, with interpretation and transformation. Situaciones doesn't work *on* new militant groups, rather they work *with* them in order to produce new knowledges, collaborative and anti-methodological knowledges, and practices from within a specific situation. The aim is to theorize what they call the "new social protagonism," the popular term to describe the wave of autonomist movements that appeared in Argentina in the late 90s and early 2000s, in a series of collaborative investigations which are published by their press Tinta Limón (www.tintalimon. org).

Situaciones' practice of militant research emerges from a critique of the three types of knowledge production that were dominant in Argentina during the late 1990s. The first is academic knowledge, which Situaciones criticizes for its reification of subjects (of research) into objects. The second is that of traditional left political parties in Argentina (the kind of left political parties one finds in parliamentary democracies, like the Green Party) which, because of their proximity to "real" life and "real" politics, like to see themselves and their relation to knowledge as superior to that of the academy. However, this approach—which always proceeds from a pre-established certainty or from the desire to make facts fit a certain set of theoretical presuppositions— is in fact no better than the academic position. The final critique is leveled against nongovernmental organizations which see the world as fundamentally static in nature and therefore approach it instrumentally, not transformatively.

Since their first series of pamphlets published in 2001, Situaciones has conducted militant research in collaboration with a staggering array of movements—not only within Argentina, with movements like the radical pedagogy initiative Universidad Trashumante and the un-occupied workers of MLN Tupamaros—but across Latin America as well, with groups like the Bolivian feminist social center and political art collective Mujeres Creando, and in Mexico with the Zapatistas. With all of these projects, Situaciones seeks to explicate the specificity of a group's particular resistance, to recuperate the multiple histories of the experiences of these groups, and to come to a common, although certainly multiple, understanding of their practice. For example, their book *19 and 20: Notes for a New Insurrection* collects a series of articles, written with or with the help of, among others, Movimiento de Trabajadores Desocupados de Solano, La Comunidad Educativa Creciendo Juntos, and the Argentine sociologist Horacio González. The book attempts to think through the "newness" of the events of December 19 and 20, 2001, the days of the popular insurrection in Argentina, and to give an explanation of how these events were lived by the groups involved. The book argues that the multitude, in this instance, was not a "constituent power" (as Hardt and Negri claim) but that the "potencias" (or the "power") of this new type of insurrection functioned in a "destituent" manner: i.e., that the events were a rupture, rather than the constitution of a new power or political subject. Whether Colectivo Situaciones is analyzing the new political subjectivities created by Argentinean social movements or the experiences and practices of a particular collective, they "develop a style of thought constituted not by the preexistence of its object, but by its interiority with respect to the phenomenon that it thinks."[4]

3

GENOCIDE IN THE NEIGHBORHOOD is a collaboration between Colectivo Situaciones and the Buenos Aires branch of the Argentinean-based human rights organization HIJOS. HIJOS, whose acronym spells out the word for "children" in Spanish (and whose ranks are constituted primarily by children of the disappeared), works, as their name indicates, to revindicate the lives of those disappeared under the Argentinean dictatorship and to fight against the systematic cultural forgetting which has been the legacy of post-dictatorship Argentina. The present book takes as its subject the "escrache," one of the practices developed by HIJOS at the end of the 1990s. HIJOS works on many different fronts, but the escrache, within the Argentinean political landscape, has been the practice that has attracted the most attention. And while HIJOS continues to organize escraches to this day, the highpoint of the practice occurred around 1999–2003, or during the moment of wide-spread new social protagonism. The translation that you hold in your hands presents a selection of the material contained in the original book. Edits were made with the consultation of Colectivo Situaciones and the only parts that have been excised from the original were an introduction to the small press that Situaciones had founded to print the book and a short text by HIJOS entitled "Documento de la Comisión de escrache de HIJOS" (Document of the Commission of the Escrache of HIJOS). The first text was removed because the current translation is not an introduction to

---

[4] Colectivo Situaciones, *19 y 20 Apuntes para el nuevo protagonismo social*, Buenos Aries: Tinta Limón 2002, 9.

Situaciones' publishing project and the second because it was very time and context specific and the translators felt it would be near impossible to re-create that context for the current readership.

The book is divided into two conversations, which are prefaced by two sets of hypotheses (written by Situaciones) that serve as the basis for the ensuing discussions. In between the two conversations is a text written by HIJOS and at the book's end is a closing statement written by Situaciones. In each conversation, the participants are identified by their group's name, not their individual names, following the convention of the original manuscript. The first conversation is between Situaciones and HIJOS. The second is between Situaciones and the Mesa de Escrache Popular. The Mesa de Escrache is a group composed of a wider range of persons and collectives than HIJOS (although it includes members of HIJOS) that began to take on a more prominent role in the organizing and operation of the escraches in 2000–2001. The second conversation explains in more detail the role of the Mesa and how it changed in important ways both HIJOS's method of working and the escrache itself. The book, taken as a whole, is a meditation on the escrache as a new type of protest founded on the idea of social condemnation and the ways in which the escrache has redefined the horizon of possibilities of political struggle.

In order to be able to describe how the escrache has transformed political practice, we need to give a little context, which necessitates a quick detour through Argentinean history. Generally speaking, recent Argentinean history can be divided into three periods: the dictatorship (1976–1983), the democratic period (1983–1990), and the neoliberal period that begins during the presidency of Carlos Menem (1991). It was during Jorge Rafael Videla's military government (which began in 1976) that programmatic, state-sponsored violence (known as The Dirty War, or la Guerra Sucia) was carried out against the Argentinean people, mainly targeting those suspected of having leftist sympathies. During the period 1973 to 1983, an estimated 30,000 people were "disappeared" as Argentinean security forces and death squads worked hand-in-hand with other South American dictatorships under the aegis of the CIA-backed Operation Condor. The military juntas that ruled Argentina until 1983, developed an entire infrastructure of hospitals, military bases, and trained personal that were used to, in essence, commit state-sponsored murder in a brutal attempt to cleanse Argentina of an entire generation of the left.

In 1984, the newly-installed democratically-elected government commissioned a report to detail the repression under the dictatorship. This report, issued by the Comisión Nacional Sobre la Desaparición de Personas (CoNaDep), was titled *Nunca Mas*, or Never Again. The conclusions of the report, which included the documentation of the disappearance of almost 9,000 persons, shocked the world. As a result of the report, in 1985, former junta leader Jorge Rafael Videla was sentenced to life imprisonment at the military prison of Magdalena.

However, the report also advanced for the first time a theory which came to be known as "theory of the two demons," and which later became the primary lens for "making sense" of the "dirty war" of the 1970s. The "theory of the two demons" was a politicized interpretation of the historical experience of the dictatorship advanced by the Unión Cívica Radical, the party in power during the "transition to democracy." The phrase attempts to cast the political struggle of the 1970s as a confrontation between two irrational demons: on the one side the militarists and on the other the left (guerillas), whose struggle held "normal society" hostage. As much as the report provided a brilliant documenting of the junta's crimes, this particular historical interpretation, wherein state-sponsored violence by a military dictatorship against the left was magically transformed into a struggle between "equals," was to have grave consequences.

As a result, Argentina's democratic government soon passed two sweeping pieces of legislation: the Ley de Punto Final and the Ley de Obediencia Debida. The Ley de Punto Final was passed in 1986 and put an end to the investigation and prosecution of people accused of political violence during the dictatorship through December 10, 1983, the day democratic rule was instituted in Argentina. The Ley de Obediencia Debida, passed in 1987, stipulated that all military and security personal could not be tried for their actions during the dictatorship as they were acting out of "due obedience." Then, in 1990, in what was seen as the ultimate affront to justice, then-president Menem issued a sweeping pardon absolving from prosecution key leaders of the National Reorganization Process (i.e. the 1976–1983 dictatorship) and certain guerillas on the grounds of "national reconciliation."

Thus, when the group HIJOS began working in the mid-1990s it was within this complicated context. The majority of the people on the left in Argentina, if they didn't have a family member who was disappeared by the government, knew someone who did and thus there was an overwhelming sense of betrayal, injustice, and complete whitewashing of a decade of state-sponsored terror. The specific legal battles around impunity for the dictatorship became more complicated as the 1990s progressed, thanks to Baltasar Garzón, a Spanish judge, who was responsible for investigating and bringing to trial, via extradition, many members of the Argentinean dictatorship, and whose work during the late 1990s re-opened the possibility of legal redress for crimes committed during the dictatorship.

As this book discusses, in the run up to the massive, widespread protests on December 19 and 20, 2001, the escraches fueled and fed off of the spread of a multitude of radical collectives and innovative social movements across Argentina. The popular uprising of December 19 and 20, 2001 was brought on, in part, by the desperate economic crisis faced by the country, a crisis that resulted from the neoliberal economic policies of the Menem and De la Rúa governments. For two days, Argentineans took to the streets in an unprecedented manner, and as these days marked the return of people en masse to the streets of Buenos Aires, they are referred to as the real end of the dictatorship, which, throughout its existence, had enforced a curfew with severe penalties. However, the escrache as a practice began primarily as a response to Menem's pardons, the Ley de Punto Final and the Ley de Obediencia Debida.

Like all truly innovative practices, what the escrache *is* is rather difficult to define: it's something between a march, an action or happening, and a public shaming. The escraches are a transformation of traditional forms of protest and were developed as a means to address two problems. The first was that of "impunity"; the second was the loss or suppression of historical memory that this legal reality created.

The escrache, then, as a practice looks like this: HIJOS selects someone to be escrached who during the dictatorship was responsible for or complicit with the torture and murder of people. When they first started, HIJOS targeted high-ranking members of the dictatorship, who primarily lived in the center of Buenos Aires. Later a decision was made to escrache lower-ranking members in part to begin to work in other parts of the city, but also to demonstrate that members of the dictatorship were everywhere living as if nothing had happened. Once a genocidist is decided upon, a date for the escrache is fixed and members from HIJOS and other related organizations spend months working in the neighborhood where this person lives; they work with neighborhood organizations and go door-to-door to discuss with individual residents and families what that person did and the need for denouncing it. They also discuss the theory and practice of the escraches. Next comes months of flyering, in order to invite and secure the participation of the residents of the neighborhood in the march, which is part of the culminating action of the escrache. The march leads the neighbors to the criminal's home where there are then theatre performances and a symbolic "painting" of the house. This "painting" usually involves throwing paint "bombs" or balloons at the building in order to mark it as the genocidist's place of residence. The idea is once again to transform the space of the neighborhood, to make visible that genocidists still walk free.[5]

The point of this transformation of public space, which also includes graffiting, stenciling, and postering through-

---

[5] Video representations of the escraches miss how they are transformative of subjectivity; they fail to give the viewer a sense of what being caught up in one is like. However, they can be useful to demonstrate the escrache's context, scope, and implementation. To this end, we recommend the following videos. The first demonstrates the carnivalesque atmosphere of the escrache, the transformation of public space through graffiti and stencils, and the composition of the crowd (neighborhood members, students, and members of Madres de la Plaza de Mayo) and the dramatic conclusion as the escrache arrives at the house of the genocidist (www.youtube.com/watch?v=26Nx7SVKTb0). The second shows the tactics used by the police to repress or impede the progress of the escrache (www.youtube.com/watch?v=8ZG798nebUU). Police and government repression of the escraches has been a constant from day one. The final video is by Etcétera, one of the artistic collectives that worked to create the escraches (www.youtube.com/watch?v=LgYsacLxo_k). The video demonstrates the tactic of using a performance in front of the genocidist's house to create confusion and to distract the police so the paint bombs can be thrown to mark the house.

out the neighborhood denouncing the presence of a genocidist, is two-fold: first, to create a new type of justice in a form of what HIJOS has termed "social condemnation." The crux is, as a member of HIJOS says in one conversation, "to turn the neighborhood into a prison," meaning that "tomorrow, the shop owner won't sell to him; the taxi-driver won't pick him up; the baker will choose not to wait on him; the paperboy will refuse to deliver the newspaper." Social condemnation is a way of rethinking justice, making it less about seeking legal reparations and more about the reconstruction of the social fabric that was destroyed by the dictatorship's actions. Thus, the escrache reactivates historical memory, using it for transformative ends.

Unlike traditional protests, the escrache is not addressed to the state but rather to a specific, local context and public: the members of the neighborhood. The escrache is not organized around the idea of reparations, or anything that eventually would come from the state or any other power. Rather the escrache escapes from the "logic of negotiation" and "representation" and posits a self-affirming idea of justice akin to Paolo Virno's concept of "exodus."[6] The escrache isn't looking to bring the government to the bargaining table or to force it to recognize that atrocities were committed. The escrache doesn't seek redress. It doesn't appeal to a higher authority. The escrache, if done well, is a form of justice in and of itself. As well, the escraches seek to put an end to the dictatorship's control of social and public space, to bring people out of their homes again, to place them

---

[6] Virno writes that exodus can be understood as "a radical politics that does not want to construct a new state. In the end, it is only that and, then, is far from the model of the revolutions that want to take power, to construct a new state, a new monopoly of political decision; to the contrary, it is—in every case—to defend power, not to take power" (from interview available at www.generation-online.org/p/fpvirno2.htm).

in relation to one another, to bring them into a collective that is more than just a community and less than a political party. The escraches militate against and work to displace the climate of suspicion, silence, and fear that characterized Argentine society under the dictatorship.

The escrache is also part procession and frequently, depending on the mood of the crowd and participation of certain artist groups, part carnival. The escrache, as Situaciones mentions in one of the conversations, is a machine for the production and transformation of subjectivity. Similar to a medieval carnival when the world was turned upside down for a day, people come to the escraches as workers, students, or neighbors, but they leave as something else. Unlike a political party, which gives you a fixed identity and a series of lines to toe, the escrache is an open-ended, transformative practice. As a result, the response to it has been enormous. Students, neighbors, children of the disappeared, workers, people from all walks of life have turned out in massive numbers to participate in the escraches. HIJOS has become so successful as an organization that there are now 16 branches outside of Argentina in countries like Guatemala and Mexico, where there are also histories of state-sponsored violence that have been whitewashed into oblivion.

The government response to the escraches from the beginning has been one of repression. The response from the right has been more complicated. On the one hand, groups on the right have attempted to appropriate the escrache for their own ends, but without the same success because they have treated it as just another form of protest, and thus miss what makes the escraches of HIJOS unique and important (i.e., the commitment to working in a neighborhood, working with the specific conditions, histories, and experiences of that situation). The second response, which has gained more traction, fueled both by the government and the media, has been the attempt to effect guilt by association and tag the escraches with a "fascist" label. The conversations in the book directly respond to this critique, so I'll let them do the work of responding. In general, however, these attacks rely on a stripping away of the specific historical and political context of the term "fascist" in order to attach a content to it which is frequently the opposite of what the term actually refers to. A more interesting approach to discussing the escraches would be to read them against other practices around popular justice or practices in Latin America that are also concerned with the construction of new types of justice. For example, the practices of the indigenous Policia Communitaria in the Mexican state of Guerrero (www.policiacomunitaria.org), which does not seek redress or the recognition of wrongs from the state, but which is creating practices which redefine and force us to reconsider the very concept of "justice" and how it is enacted institutionally in contemporary society.

As the conversations here discuss at great length, the escrache does not seek to seize state power, whether through elections or by other means. HIJOS and the other groups that participate in the escraches have been very clear about this. The point is not one day to become popular enough to form a party. The escrache, obviously then, derives a good deal of its force from the fact that it steps outside traditional political logics and addresses a sentiment that many have felt for some time—namely, a dissatisfaction with "party politics." The escrache participates in a new idea of the political—a politics that produces new subjectivities, creates another idea of time, and activates the potential in a given situation. The escrache offers a strong critique of the deferral that characterizes party politics ("when we take power...") and the commitment to the logic of negotiation that questing for the state requires. The escraches emphatically demonstrate that another politics is possible.

Another aspect of the escrache that we want to mention, which is not really discussed at length in this book but has received a great deal of attention, is the participation of artistic collectives like Grupo Arte Callejero and Etcéctera in the creation of the escraches. Within artistic circles, the participation of these groups has been much discussed, in part because of the way in which the escrache has an affinity with techniques from avant-garde artistic traditions. The escraches heavily involve the transformation of public space via postering, stenciling, and graffiti. Thus, the escrache is not just a form of protest but also a machine of semiotic production. It is a form of protest that both produces its own imaginary and that transforms the spaces that it transverses. The escraches also involve a great deal of performance, during the marches and as their culmination. In many respects, this is a happening, politicized and taken to the streets. Indeed many artists and critics in Europe and the United States have seen the escraches as (finally) the realization of the political aspirations of the most radical forms of performance art: a practice that activates the political potentialities in a given situation. And while there is something to this reading, it smacks of the wishful thinking that continues to masquerade as political engagement in the commercialized art world.

The escraches form part of a number of new practices and experiences that were taking place in the late 90s, early 00s in Argentina. Many of these practices involved artistic collectives in new and radical ways, and this moment saw the flourishing of a series of brilliant groups (Arde Arte!, Taller Popular de Serigrafia, Grupo Arte Callejero, and Etcétera, to name a few) who developed practices that took place completely outside artistic institutions. Unfortunately, the process of translating this work and bringing it into a broader US art world context is only just beginning. The importance of the way artistic collectives and techniques of semiotic production became a key part of the escrache is two-fold. First, instead of the production of commodities or dematerialized works within a gallery or institutional setting, here we have artistic collectives deciding to work directly with social movements. These collectives like Grupo Arte Callejero, and Etcétera went to the escraches and asked "what's possible here?" And through a long process of trial and discovery they produced a practice that escaped the merely aesthetic and became a political practice. Second, this is not institutional critique or relational aesthetics; it is a pointed, direct, highly critical refusal of the limited politics both of these positions offer. The escrache is an exodus from the art institution in favor of looking for new ways of working, new ways of activating "artistic" traditions towards political ends. The escrache, then, is a transversal line that cuts across the specific histories of avant garde movements and political groups and concatenates them into new assemblages, new figures, new forms. This is both its power and its legacy.

4

I'D LIKE NOW to introduce a few concepts that inform the thinking of Colectivo Situaciones and which might be useful for reading the text that follows. However, I do so with the following caveat: there's a danger in introducing the book via theoretical precepts. If the book is read as being an elaboration of some pre-established theoretical formula or position, this would be a grave misreading. This book emerges out of the "putting into a situation of a hypothesis"; it is a test of what a collaborative process of knowledge production can create. The point is to overcome the gap between theory and practice, investigator and investigated, in order to produce some unruly third thing, or a knowledge that would escape from all of these binaries.

The motivation in introducing these terms is only to clarify some of the ideas that form the background of the work but remain latent in the text itself. We have to be careful here because such a philosophic presentation runs the risk of setting this work up to be measured against standards that it would refuse, and, what's more, standards that would seriously distort the intent of this book, which is the production of not just knowledge, but knowledge and action.

With this in mind, three ideas are fundamental to understanding the practice of Situaciones: situation, potencia, and counterpower. Situation, obviously given the name alone, is a key term for the group, one which initiated and continues to define their practice. The term situation is a way of defining their project against the objective distance of academic work and the instrumental knowledge generated by left parties. Situation is a site from which to think and intervene; a site which would be neither one of totality nor one that accepts abstraction as the basis of knowledge. Working in a situation means thinking and doing at the same time. Situation, then, is a site for work that aims to be immanent to the practices under study.[7]

For Situaciones, the operative idea is not that of practices or theories to be studied but rather situations within which one thinks and out of which one acts. Ideas are not

---

[7] The use of this term derives neither from Negri nor Debord, both of whom have radically different approaches to the idea, but rather from a diverse array of thinkers, experiences, and chance. As Colectivo Situaciones wrote in response to queries about this term: "Thus, Badiou, Miguel Benasayag, Sartre, own our experiences of breaking with traditional forms of political organization and social investigation, plus the idea of singularity from Deleuze and so many other influences, always partial . . . In the end, a mélange, nothing definable in any clear way. And in general this has to do with the fact that we are always uncomfortable when people begin describing us as 'followers of . . . .' "

applied to objects, but rather meaning emerges from concrete experience and the discussion of it in a process that unfolds in complicated ways across various levels of experience. The work of the militant researcher is to faithfully trace and live this process or unfolding.

The idea of potencia derives more directly from contemporary political theory, specifically from Antonio Negri's discussion, first given in *The Savage Anomaly*, of the distinction in Spinoza between "potestas" (the power of the sovereign) and "potentia" (the immanent capability or potentiality of life itself). Spanish, as with most Romance languages, preserves a similar distinction between "poder" and "potencia." Situaciones takes full advantage of this distinction, up to the point where they have described their work, and that of research militancy in general, as simply the activation of the potencia in any given situation.[8] For Situaciones, poder is always the fixing of a force, while potencia is what is produced by social relations or what emerges from the "material encounter of bodies." Poder is a fixed power, like a state. Potencia is the escrache. They write:

> . . . how to work from the power (potencia) of what is and not of what "ought to be" (ideal)? Above all, when the ideal is a more or less arbitrary and personal projection to which nobody has necessarily to adapt. Research militancy does not extract its commitment from a model of the future, but from a search for power (potencia) in the present. That is why the most serious

---

[8] For a more in-depth discussion of this distinction, see Holdren and Touza, "Introduction to Colectivo Situaciones," *ephemera* 5:4.

> fight is against the "a priori," against predefined
> schemes.[9]

FOR SITUACIONES, THE shift from poder to potencia opens up the possibility of thinking a politics beyond the state. Theirs is a refusal of left party politics-as-usual in favor of a volatile, highly engaged relationship to the present, which theorizes itself as not just detournement of what is but as an activation of new forms and powers (potencias) of resistance which are latent within any given context.

What is unique and interesting about Situaciones' approach is their respect for the particular, for concrete experience. This is what allows them to abandon power (poder) as the interlocutor for political action. Moreover, their approach allows us to think about the importance of many experiences that break with or evidence a disinterest in the traditional left obsession with taking state power and that have been consequently depreciated for their supposed "lack of politics" (such a critique of HIJOS is discussed at length in the first conversation).

This brings us then to our third and final term, counterpower—a term that Situaciones has devoted an entire book to discussing.[10] Essentially, counterpower is a theory of how groups with no interest in seizing state power can have transformative effects. A counterpower is a revolutionary activity that never crystallizes as a "new power" (that is a fixed power, a poder) but which works transversally across

---

[9] Colectivo Situaciones, "Something More on Research Militancy: Footnotes on Procedures and (In)Decisions," trans. Nate Holdren and Sebastian Touza, *ephemera* 5: 4 (November 2005): 602-614.

[10] *Contrapoder: Una Introducción.* Buenos Aries:Tinta Limón, 2001.For more information on this book, see www.tintalimon.com.ar/spip.php?article8. Contributors include Colectivo Situaciones, Toni Negri, John Holloway, Miguel Benasayag, Luis Matini, Horacio González, and Ulrich Brandt.

the state and capitalist institutions to create new social formations and to activate potencias. Counterpower is then a description of how social movements, even when they are uninterested in taking state power, can still constitute effective responses to state power. The Zapatistas are exemplary in this respect, as they demonstrate both theoretically and practically that "politics no longer passes through the political."[11]

5

WHAT COULD THIS book mean in the United States? I hope this book will encourage a serious engagement with autonomist practices by activists, artists, writers, and the public at large. We are living in the midst of a massive restructuring of capital, the realization that what follows the neoliberal nightmare which stripped away the last of government protections for everyone except big business is not something better, but rather the institutionalization of permanent crisis (or crisis, the final frontier of value in disaster capitalism). If we want nontoxic food, health care, affordable education, housing, an environment not on the verge of catastrophe collapse . . . if we want any of these things, they will have to be fought for. And it is my belief that the now lengthy history of autonomist practices can speak to this dire situation we find ourselves in.

By making the ideas in this book available in English, we hope for a rethinking of militancy in the United States. We have to radicalize both our politics and our ways of living. We have to communize ourselves and our communities to create livable worlds in the cracks of disaster capitalism. And this means throwing off NGO models and rethinking what it might mean to work in and with "communities"

---

[11] *ibid*, 32.

in a way that is not ultimately reactionary, in a way that does more than just "manage" crisis. It means thinking outside political party structures and not turning to the state at every juncture to solve our problems. The escrache, while not a solution by itself (obviously) to any of these problems, will hopefully be a spur to both thought and action. The issue is not one of translating the practice, of figuring out how we can do escraches here, but rather of spirit: how can we build practices that would be adequate to our contemporary situation, as the escrache was to its own.

Many of our friends disagreed with our decision to translate this particular book. Some felt other books by Colectivo Situaciones, something other than their first book (which is really just a pamphlet) would be more representative of their work. Others felt that the book was overly specific, too tied to its Argentinean context to be read profitably in the United States. For us, however, this book had an attraction that we could not deny. Right at the moment when we were despairing of the possibility of a politics post-9/11 with the "end" of the antiglobalization movement, this book fell into our laps. It was at a time when the universality demanded by current "left" political theory (Zizek, Badiou) seemed hubristic, when de-linking action and militancy from the state seemed to make a great deal of sense.

While the book doesn't address any of the big "what can be done" questions directly, it reminds us not just of the dangers of melancholy but also that the project of inventing political practices that match the contemporary moment is an on-going and entirely essential venture. As Situaciones write in this book, "The escraches are, first, a call to struggle, a practical confirmation that transformative action exists now or not at all." *Genocide in the Neighborhood* shows us how powerfully transformative *and* affirmative practices such as the escrache can be. Above all, we want to be, in every way but especially in our politics, on the side of life; we want to *affirm*.

As stated above, what is important to us about militant research as a practice is its insistence on the significance of the particulars of experience, overcoming the abyss between theory and practice, and its commitment to "thinking" and "theorizing" simultaneously with transformative action. This consideration, care, and respectful positioning vis a vis lived experience in Situaciones' work is most powerfully expressed in *Genocide in the Neighborhood*. There are highly important critiques in the book, ones that we feel really resonate in the US context; for example, critiques of the limits of institutional justice, of the limits of militant activity within the state, and of a kind of melancholic irony that is a common affective state in the face of grim political realities. However, what really touched a nerve in this book—what has really stayed with us—has been this radical attention to what Situaciones term *situation*. All possible transformative action resides here in a kind of temporal locality. Transformative action is, in part, a matter of understanding and activating the potential in a given situation. For those of us trapped inside the overwhelming spectacularization of experience, or even better the spectacularization of non-events that so marks our contemporary experience, this approach appeals to us on a number of levels.

Finally, for those of us interested in rethinking the connections between art and politics, the escrache as a practice, as one that fulfills so many previously "unrealizable" desires or that makes possible so many new concatenations of art and politics, helps us to imagine ways that we might rethink our own practices and what we can ask from them. It should also force us to consider how we engage with institutions, how we constitute and reproduce organizations of sociality, and what the limits of our critiques and practices are. Obviously, direct action is not always the answer, but to come up with a better way of working or thinking, with practices that attempt to not merely describe but transform, with practices that don't just fall into the easy acceptance of things as they are (or even worse that grandstand as "truly political" while remaining merely aesthetic)—this is the task for today. Perhaps, to put it more simply, if politics today is truly "nothing other than the realization of new forms of making and understanding social life," the escraches and this book can help restore a certain kind of faith in the necessity of critical artistic practice. It has done so for us.

THE ESCRACHES OF HIJOS: REASONS AND MOTIVES

Colectivo Situaciones

WE DON'T HAVE a predetermined set of motives, and perhaps we could have started from somewhere else. The experiences that we want to discuss in our upcoming books are many.[1] Nevertheless, the decision to begin with the escraches of HIJOS was unanimous. Unanimous and spontaneous. Our reasons for beginning here can't be enumerated: a list would never be able to explain the mark that the escraches of HIJOS have left—on us at least.

Although we could start with the affinity that unites us with them. In one sense, HIJOS are our friends and compañeros; but in another sense—one more profound and more binding—they are our brothers.

But there's more. Namely, how they live politics and the radical demand they make of history. This is something that we admired from the start. The escraches of HIJOS have a

---

[1] *Trans.* For a full list of books that Colectivo Situaciones has published since *Genocide in the Neighborhood*, please visit their website www.situaciones.org or that of their press www.tintalimonediciones.org.

dynamic and a force that overwhelms. To pass through one of these unique protests is to experience physical and spiritual intensities that are rarely equaled. HIJOS inspires us.

There are other reasons as well. The escraches of HIJOS constitute a whole that easily surpasses the sum of its parts; that is, the group HIJOS and the escraches. What moves us, then, is this combination. A mixture of adolescent rebellion with the eternal return of a shattered history that is, at the same time, a repetition and a making-new.

These intuitions were the ones that we tried to put down on paper, as if they were real theses, to be worked on with HIJOS. These intuitions, we believe, were present during a long conversation that we had one rainy Friday night in September in an old house formerly used by anarchist groups.

Once immersed in conversation, we had the feeling that HIJOS hadn't turned on their tape recorder. They were ready for something to emerge, something like a collective thought. This was not a simple interview for us nor was it for them. It was an opportunity to think together, to write each other. Afterwards, the conversation was edited and read by both groups but only to correct redundancies and cut out interruptions that added little to the exchange. We have strictly respected the movement of the dialogue, its digressions, its twists and turns, because we believe that here, in the movement of the thought, lies the key to what occurred that night.

This book, needless to say, is dedicated to our comrades, the 30,000 disappeared. But not as part of an unrecoverable past, nor as part of a sad memory, nor as a requiem for the victims. We have had enough of that in our country. If there is something that we share with HIJOS it is that the past is not something "already past," something which has been left behind forever, but that the past is here, in each escrache, and that the struggle of these revolutionaries—the disappeared and those that survive—is our struggle. This is not an homage, rather just a decision to continue on the path towards justice and freedom.

THE ESCRACHES: 9 HYPOTHESES FOR DISCUSSION

colectivo situaciones

1

THE ESCRACHES EXCEED the traditional forms of politics: they are a novel practice that affirms a new sense of politics and of militancy.

In this sense, it's critical to begin to scrutinize it and draw out its implications. Like the Zapatista experience, that of the Brazilian Landless Workers' Movement[1] and many others, the escrache creates[2] a new revolutionary

---

[1] *Trans.* The Movimento dos Trabalhadores Rurais Sem Terra (MST) is an important Brazilian social movement with more than 1.5 million members that focuses on land reform and land redistribution. They are best known for their practice of organizing landless families to seize underused farmland, which they begin to live on and farm. This practice is a direct challenge to the structure of property ownership in Brazil, where 3% of the population owns two-thirds of all arable lands.

[2] *Trans.* Throughout this section Colectivo Situaciones uses the verb *fundar* in connection with the escrache, which we have alternately translated as "to create" and "to found." *To found,* in the sense of both "taking the first steps in building" and "establishing with a provision for future maintenance," is closest to the meaning

subjectivity. To think what the escrache signifies and to delineate its actual characteristics is the only way to prevent its interpretation via formulas that today no longer have any currency. This is the objective of this encounter.

2

THE ESCRACHES ARE, first, a call to struggle, a practical confirmation that transformative action exists now or not at all. They are the opposite of the melancholy of those that wait, seated, for a better world. The escrache shows us that struggle doesn't depend on the idea of a glorious tomorrow, on a scientifically demonstrated strategy, nor on a savior who will descend and liberate us.

Because of this, the escrache creates a different idea of time, different than that offered to us by capitalism.

For capitalism, the past is already gone, it only exists as passive memory, as *Never Again*. The future is a far-away, vague promise that doesn't depend on us. As such, our present is weak, sad: we are alone, awaiting a miracle.

In the escrache, on the contrary, the past acts forcefully; the disappeared live in the present. It is a past that affirms that it is a past of the present. Moreover, the future has already arrived, because it is nothing other than that which we are constructing, that which depends on us: it is the future of the present. Thus, the escrache founds a present, decisive and full of potentialities.

The escrache is a practice that neither waits nor conforms. It appears today and is for now.

---

of *fundar*, and we have used it wherever usage permits. In all other instances, we have used the slightly more ephemeral, but serviceable, *to create*.

3

THIS IS SO, because the escrache only exists as a response to the demand for JUSTICE, the demand that founds it. It is this necessity that it affirms in practice. And it's a demand that requires no justification. It doesn't need a theoretical apparatus, nor individual adherents; it does not depend on "consensus."

It is a truth independent of the complexity of the present moment, of the logic of the State, of relations of power, and it is not exhausted by any reparation. The escrache refuses to be simply a representation of victims and thus it doesn't seek a solution in Power.

The escrache generates a militant commitment, one that always moves beyond, that does not depend on power. It is a new sense of commitment.

4

THE ESCRACHE CREATES a different idea and practice of justice, one opposed and antagonistic to formal justice. And with this new justice, it founds a new practice and concept of democracy.

First, "if there is no justice, there is escrache."[3] Justice doesn't depend on an institution that embodies it, but on an action that produces it. It is not the institution, the norm, nor even human rights that founds the just, but the act and the concrete practice of justice.

Second, and most importantly, the search for justice does not end with imprisonment nor can it be contained in legal bureaucracies. The struggle expressed by the escrache goes beyond the State of Rights and can't be reabsorbed by

---

[3] *Trans.* This was the first slogan of HIJOS. For a more in depth discussion see p. 162 of this volume.

it. If one, two, or ten of the military genocidists were in prison today, the escraches wouldn't cease.

The escrache creates a new idea of justice founded in the popular capacity for producing truths that power is not able to neutralize via cooptation.[4] It is in this practice that "the people" becomes an autonomous subject.

5

THE ESCRACHE, THEN, is a situation; one that proposes and implements an alternative practice, one that contains the hints of a new society. However, these hints are revealed in the escrache independently of the slogans or phrases that we use to interpret it. In fact, sometimes we even use language that is contrary to what we practice; as when, for example, we ask the State for justice at the same moment that we deny this justice and found another.

This contradiction demonstrates something funda-mental: the subject of politics is the situation in which we participate, the collective action to which we are commit-ted, and not us as isolated individuals or the ideas that we might have about our practice.

---

[4] *Trans.* The Spanish adjective *popular*, as used here, is difficult to render into English. The most direct translation, "popular," lacks the sense of collectivity one hears in the Spanish. Instead of in-dicating that something is liked or sought after by many people, *capacidad popular* signifies "the capacity of a group of people," wherein it is understood that this capacity is somehow inherent to the group. A similar problem occurs in the following sentence with *el campo popular*, which we have chosen to render as "the people" with quotes in the hopes of mitigating the outdated over-tones the phrase carries, and which the Spanish definitively does not have (although more for cultural rather than linguistic rea-sons). Rather the adjective in Spanish would seem to indicate a different (and perhaps more positive) way of thinking about the potential inherent within any collectivity or group.

As a result, the escrache functions like a machine. It does not matter how many people participate in it, nor how it was organized. When it begins to act, it works with an infectious radicality: it shakes up the neighborhood and spontaneously incorporates people.

6

THE CONTRIBUTION AND importance of the escrache is singular, specific. It is the search for justice and nothing more. It is because of this (and not in spite of it) that it is so powerful. Because of this it is also universal; and it is via this singularity that we feel a part of it and we feel expressed within it.

It would be a mistake if tomorrow HIJOS began preaching about what workers should be doing, or about the strategies that the squatters should follow, or about how scientists should conduct their investigations. If HIJOS are a part of the vanguard today, it is because they make escraches. And not because they give advice.

The escrache shows us that the vanguards of today are defined by their concrete practices and not by their opinions. And it also shows that all political practice, be it vanguard, alternative, or revolutionary is singular and situated.

7

THE SINGULARITY OF the escrache of HIJOS is confirmed in another way. Often, when the escrache is adopted by others, it loses its profound significance and, thus, its radical political edge. This has occurred with unions, political parties, and university groups who have used escraches to ask for higher salaries, a larger budget, etc. from the powers-that-be, be it a state power or not. On these occasions, the essence of the escrache is lost, trapped within the logic of negotiation.

It is evident that the political significance of the escrache, its universality, lies somewhere other than in its facile imitation.

8

Hijos is a social movement that is organized around a demand for justice. It was in response to this concrete demand that the escrache, a practice that founds a new way of understanding justice, was invented. The escrache, because of this, is political. And politics then is nothing other than the realization of new forms of making and understanding social life.

This is the opposite of understanding politics as something other than social struggle; for example, as a fight for magnificent abstractions, for "liberty," "the revolution," or "the good of humanity," abstractions that will only be realized (perhaps) when we take power.

Politics is the realization of transformational projects and not the elaboration of well-planned and pre-approved programs. HIJOS makes the escraches, while the parties of the left try to capitalize on it (for their "important" strategy). Because of this, HIJOS rejects the parties of the left.

HIJOS is a political organization because it is not a party and doesn't pretend to be one.

9

The escrache is then a new practice of transformation. Once it is seen like this, we can encounter thousands of experiences that share its desire—experiences perhaps less spectacular, less well-known or less often cited, but equally as important. They are situations of resistance and of new forms of existence: situations where autonomous forms of existence (which are different than those of Power) are produced and then spread to every area of life.

The deepening and unfolding of these experiences and the capacity that they have for mutually reinforcing each other is the site of revolutionary politics today.

COLECTIVO SITUACIONES
IN CONVERSATION WITH HIJOS

SEPTEMBER 8, 2000

HIJOS:[1] I'D LIKE to discuss the third hypothesis where it says, "The escrache is organized as a response to the demand that creates it, it doesn't need a finished program, nor even individual adherents, it doesn't depend on consensus, it doesn't depend on relations of power." I don't think it's really like that.

And the other point to discuss is hypothesis four, the idea of what would happen to the escrache if there was some type of justice. I'm not so certain that nothing would

---

[1] *Trans.* In the following transcription, speakers are only listed (as they are in the original) by their representative group: HIJOS or Colectivo Situaciones. Thus, frequently, several speakers from HIJOS will follow one another and sometimes members of the same group will be in disagreement or will contradict one another. This way of presenting the text, as a conversation between collectives, and as a text that preserves the twists and turns of that conversation and the disagreements, and hesitations therein, is an integral part of Colectivo Situationes' critical and research practice, which focuses on the collaborative generation of knowledge from within a *situation.*

happen, that everything would be the same, that it'd have the same effect, the same radicality that you mention, the same shock. Obviously, like you say, if two, three, ten military genocidists are imprisoned it doesn't change the situation, because there are already, more or less, that number in prison. Tiger Acosta is in Campo de Mayo, Massera has been put away.[2] So, in this case, no, but if it was a type of justice that society perceived as more real. . . . This is linked to the fact that, for me, the escrache definitely depends on consensus and relations of power.

Situaciones: I don't understand the idea of relations of power as you're posing it. What you're saying sounds pretty debatable to me. Let's say all the soldiers were prisoners, wouldn't there be escraches for the journalists, priests who were complicit with the dictatorship. . . . And if they were all prisoners, wouldn't we start in on the corporations? And where would we stop? Because in the end, where does the collaboration with the dictatorship stop? I mean what would need to happen so that we can say "there was justice" is something representative justice—the justice of the system—just can't do.

But the other point seems to me more difficult to understand, the idea of relations of power. What are you proposing?

---

[2] *Trans.* Jorge (Tiger) Acosta was one of most notorious torturers at the infamous Navy School of Mechanics, implicated in the theft of babies from women killed in secret torture centers during the 1976–83 dictatorship. Emilio Eduardo Massera played an important role in the 1976 coup d' état against Isabel Perón and was then named head of the military junta set up to rule Argentina. In 1983, he was tried for human rights violations and sentenced to life in prison. However, in 1990, he was pardoned by then-President Carlos Menem.

H: That, for me, the escrache does depend on some type of consensus and desires for a consensus. I don't know if it's a consensus understood only in a particular way, but it's definitely a moral condemnation . . . the escrache expands what "passing judgment" might mean. If it's not seen as having this expansive effect, it seems as if it doesn't matter if there's consensus and that we would just do it anyway. But the escrache is done in order to change the perception of many people, and that's what you're saying [in the thesis]: that the impunity is something of the present, concrete, that the effects of the dictatorship are ongoing.[3] The escrache is done to make them see that this is a guy who, in that time, acted, repressed people, and today is still free.

Because of this, it does depend on consensus. Or, that is, I don't know if you would say this, I'm not sure, but for me the escrache depends profoundly on a social condemnation. If you get 2,000 people to an escrache, it's not the same as if there's 50. For us, it's not the same; for the neighborhood it's not the same.

I don't know what everyone else thinks, but to me it seems like the escrache by itself, poorly done that is, without all the work that's behind it. . . . It's not just that there are soldiers,[4] or that you don't need to explain anything when you do an escrache. It's not this that distinguishes ours from other escraches, which have bastardized the form or which, for us, are just bogus. The difference is not just in who is being escrached, but in all the labor, in the seriousness with which it's undertaken. That is, it's not opportunism,

---

[3] *Trans.* "Impunity" here refers to the Ley de Punto Final and the Ley de Obediencia Debida discussed in the editor's introduction on p. 18.

[4] *Trans.* This is a reference to the repression the escraches faced from the police and how soldiers would block the route and encircle the house to be escrached.

it's something that you achieve bit by bit. We worry about each element of the escrache. When the murga fails, for us, the escrache fails.[5] It's an essential part. In the last few escraches, where there wasn't a murga, the music got louder, the people stopped talking, and it was like a procession. The escrache is people amped up, people who are full of energy, and, for me, this is also what gives it its authenticity.

S: For us as well, and precisely because of this we don't see the escrache as existing within the framework of consensus, because consensus would mean that other people agree with what you're doing. And HIJOS, it seems to me, is working in an area that is not that of opinion, in an area where it doesn't matter that much what other people might think, rather you place into motion a dynamic that questions the logic of pure opinion, which, in the end, is the logic of representative democracy: "Well, I think this is best, I'll go and vote for it, ciao" and do nothing more. The escraches don't let you act like this, you have to take responsibility for what's there, to know that there can be repression, and you get a different level of confrontation, and that's where all of that energy that you mentioned is.

And the fact that you don't need justification is because, in the final analysis, you are questioning many elements of

---

[5] *Trans.* The murga is a type of street-based musical theatre performed during carnival; it has its roots in Uruguay but is also found in Buenos Aires and in other locations in the Rio de la Plata region. A murga, generally speaking, is a group that performs a suite of songs and dances whose themes are drawn either from everyday life or the events of the prior year (depending on the performance context). The murga was a tradition that was explicitly targeted by the Argentinean dictatorship, which came close to banning carnival and murga groups. The murga as a popular tradition in Argentina, experienced a significant resurgence during the middle of the 1990s.

the dominant consensus in Argentina which created this situation where there is no justice. Even if in the escraches the whole world gets to say how good it would be if the generals were prisoners, consensus is not an element that makes the escrache possible—because the escraches would be done anyway, right? At least that's how it seems to me, but you tell me what you think. As much as the escrache has predetermined objectives, the idea that we have of it is that when it ends something has happened, independently of what effect it might have later. Although the effect could be good or bad, when the escrache ends something has happened. It's not that if it doesn't affect public opinion it hasn't worked, but rather that something was moved, something occurred, something was added to reality.

H: If there is not a consensus in the neighborhood, if you go a month before to talk and the people reject you, I don't know if HIJOS would continue working there; that is, if there is not a consensus in the neighborhood, in the press, among the people, among militants. I think that consensus is essential for us. Moreover, there are many people who support us and who don't see the escraches as a personal attack, as something put together by just 50 people.

S: There's an experience I can share concerning the Biblioteca Nacional, as seen from the inside. It's what happened in the Biblioteca after the famous escrache of Trimarchi. The first thing is that when people found that there was some motherfucker like him working there, hired by the library, there was a lot of anger, and, in fact, 40 out of the 300 people that work at the library went to the escrache. From my perspective, it wasn't like the escrache just came and went, but rather it left a really profound mark there. In fact, the managers suffered reprisals. But what changed, above all, was the feeling that arose, namely that of "I can't work with a murderer." You can work with a crook, with some asshole, but with a murderer? No one can tolerate that, it was too much.

The other moment took place during a discussion in an assembly afterwards. A militant had problems with having done the escrache and was saying that it wasn't the right moment to do it, since the director could have punished the employees, etc. The response of the assembly was that when people found out that Trimarchi worked there, it was a serious problem, a problem of impunity, and that it wasn't possible not to do the escrache, that it had to be done. It was impossible to subordinate it to a union logic, to the logic of negotiation, or to the kind of calculated stance that would use an escrache at a certain, critical moment in order to force the authorities to give up more in a negotiation.

S: What I believe is that the escrache is, in effect, beyond consensus, and in this sense doesn't depend on it. Although it's certain that the escrache came about when there was already a fairly widespread consensus in society that the militarists were motherfuckers and that it was bullshit that they were free. This is one way of thinking of it. And because of this, it seems to me that the escrache moves beyond consensus. Because the fucked-up thing about consensus, for us, is that even though the whole world says that the militarists should be prisoners, these ideas of relations of power, that democracy has to be protected, that the legal bureaucracy is impartial, makes it so that the militarists aren't in jail. Thus, in this sense, the escraches don't depend on whether tomorrow they repeal the laws of impunity.

This problem with "consensus" can be seen in many other areas. For example, they're destroying education through privatization even though there is a general consensus that it ought to be public.

I think the escrache is a concrete political practice, in which it doesn't matter if the whole world is in agreement or not. There is no justice precisely because society is founded on consensus and on relations of power. From this perspective, from a popular perspective, consensus becomes a trap, and when faced with this what can be done? Well, the escrache is one answer.

S: I think that the difference can be seen with the political parties who are against pardons. When Menem gave out his pardon, most people were against it, and perhaps continue to be against it, and certainly the majority of the political parties were against it. Now, between a politician who comes on TV saying that he doesn't want pardons and the polls that register that 85% of people are against the pardons, between this world and the escrache, there is a huge difference. For me that's crystal clear. I don't know if I'm not expressing it clearly or if it's that we really don't agree at all. The difference is that the escrache employs a direct, physical type of action that doesn't require argument and that moves directly to making justice. This is another level and gives the escrache its incredible force. It's the force of those who are in the escrache, but also of those who see it passing by or who sign a resolution in favor of it. It's really difficult to suppress an escrache—although the police could easily beat people up—but still to suppress an escrache, as all of society is looking on, is much more complicated than suppressing just any march. Because there is a force in the escrache itself that supersedes how many people say the militarists are bad or not, and this force is the switch from talking to participating, to placing the body into action and withstanding what must be withstood.

Moreover many people who work with the escraches have never reflected on or discussed much the arguments for or against them. How many people have asked themselves what are the arguments for and against the escraches?

That is, now it's not even necessary to consider all these arguments, because the escrache in itself appears as just. Thus, as a consequence, it appears necessary to go beyond representative democracy and all that. This seems like a very important part of the escrache.

S: A question. You say that the escrache is a social condemnation. Now you also say that the work leading up to the escrache is very important. The question that I'm now asking myself is this: If during this prior work you had seen that no consensus was possible, would you still do the escrache?

H: You have to.

H: But when we work without this consensus, the escraches become media-centric, and it isn't as interesting. It's tricky because it looks good, but it's really not.

H: It's that no matter what happens we're not going to renounce the escrache. Even if all of society is against it.

S: When you all thought of the escrache, when you began to talk about it, when you began to flesh out the idea of it, I imagine you didn't speculate on whether it was going to generate a consensus or not. I imagine you just decided: we have to look for a form of justice that is different, because this justice is not working. It might be that recently a consensus has formed, but not in the sense of a prior calculation, a tool to achieve a goal. Thus, it seems to me that the fact that in this neighborhood there isn't consensus, isn't going to stop the escrache. Besides, consensus is, to me at least, a horrible word: it signifies that I have to agree about what is to be done. I believe that this is what all political parties, in fact, do; "they agree," like they "agree" with the imaginary of the people.

H: I think that the escrache emerged not just from HIJOS but from within a broader context. And it came about as an alternative way of making justice. Not as an alternative owned or created by HIJOS, but as a proposal for an outside, for the people, with the idea that the people take it up, that it doesn't depend only on us. I don't know then how many times we have to talk about it to bring about a consensus, before or after. We just wanted to create an alternative justice, to mark that we were still waiting for justice, but also to move beyond ourselves, to go toward the people. Perhaps the right word isn't consensus but participation— the possibility of generating another sort of participation and political activity, in which it would be easy for other people to participate, one where they wouldn't have to go to a meeting, or become part of a group, or follow the court proceedings. We wanted to generate another possibility.

S: When we talk about consensus, I think that we're referring to this: when does a truth need consensus to be a truth and when not. For example, Obediencia Debida and the Punto Final were consensuses. In a way, they didn't count on the support of the majority, they counted on a certain repulsion. But there is a representative justice that functions (like shit, but it functions) and is based on this dynamic. Would HIJOS subordinate the truth of the escrache to the consensus of the moment, to what the media says?

H: What's happening is that you're using a definition of consensus that means agreeing with public opinion. When we speak of consensus, we're talking about coming to a place and creating an understanding about a type of action. This is very important, because there is a way of acting, a political practice, that we're pushing and the idea is that we do it with other social groups. Thus, in the Mesa de Escrache people from the neighborhood and from other groups participate in making the escrache. And that's what we're calling consensus. Perhaps there is a confusion of terms.

H: Clearly, the escrache doesn't depend on consensus in the way you are using the term. We'd do it anyway. What we point to, and what we're calling consensus here, is that the people become a part of the social condemnation.

S: Okay, now we've gotten somewhere. Consensus doesn't have anything to do with saying what it "means"—for that we could use a dictionary. To clarify the difference: in the first case, one wants to know what people think in order to do more or less what they want. While the second appeals to a more profound truth. Thus, obviously, one is lead to search for new ways of acting, because now you're not saying to the people, "and what's your opinion?" but rather, "here there is an injustice; here it's necessary to fix justice." It's a call to action. It's a call to do something that is not a part of the democracy of the political parties. I think we can now say that escraches are not just one more opinion in the world of consensus. But what this might mean is difficult to understand, for us at least.

H: Yes, what people's opinions are, what's seen on the surface, is one thing. We go deeper, or lower you might say: we work from the bottom because we don't believe in those on high. When we speak of consensus, we do it thinking about society. And we do it in a neighborhood with the idea of going to the more popular sectors. When we did several escraches in the downtown, we said, "Enough with the downtown let's go to the neighborhoods." Even though we had already done escraches many times in such areas, we returned. We had bigger targets in the center and that, in some sense, impacted the political landscape of the moment. But we voted no that that wasn't what interested us. Instead, we'll go to this son of a bitch that lives in Floresta, that no one worries about, but that lives in a zone where we can gain participation, gain adherents, mobilize, and transform the area.

H: The same thing happened with the Biblioteca Nacional, where we left but the people continued.

H: Yes, the escrache has had various stages and there are different types of escraches. One is what someone mentioned earlier, the media-centric escrache, which is set up in a day, where we and a bunch of people go to the center to find some guy who everyone knows, who could be Arguindegui or Massera.

And the other is the escrache that is above all a project in a neighborhood, talking with neighbors, hanging flyers. Here begins the escrache as we now know it. The point is that the effect is additive, the act of the escrache, the murgas, the theatre groups, and the rest of it. But the escrache is not only this, just going to the house of some guy—afterward, the escrache continues.

H: Now, I understand what you mean about the difference with other types of escraches where it's necessary to compromise on certain points, to negotiate . . . and what I hear here is that the escrache points to a truth that's not negotiable and that, at the same time, this truth has to be shared.

S: I think it's that and more. . . . This is why the escrache doesn't need to explain itself. Because the truth of consensus is what the politicians succeed in making us understand barely and only after a lot of explaining. For example, why the Obediencia Debida? They tell you that because of the relations of power, or because of democracy, because of international relations . . . they give a bunch of arguments and you still barely understand what they mean. But an escrache, on the other hand, needs very few arguments to reach everyone, not to make adherents of them, but so that everyone knows what the escrache is capable of. I think that this began with the Madres during the dictatorship when suddenly the scarf replaced years of discourse and the whole world quickly understood what it meant.[6] I think this is very different from when a militant comes around with a flyer explaining some group's program. You know, the type of person that invents argument after argument in hopes that people will finally say, "Yes, I agree with your program." The escraches are something else: you suddenly see a group of people passing, you come closer and exchange a few words, and then you know what they're talking about, because the truth of the escraches is a truth that is current for every Argentinean in some way. We need to now discuss a little bit about what the power of the escrache is—now

---

[6] Trans. The Madres de la Plaza de Mayo is an association of Argentinean mothers formed in 1977 with the purpose of tracking down and demanding the release of children who had been "detained" by the dictatorship. The Madres developed a unique form of protest which includes gathering at the Plaza de Mayo, the main square of Buenos Aires situated in front of the Casa Rosada, every Thursday in a silent protest, which they have done for the last 20 years. During these gatherings, the Madres wear white scarves, which have come to serve as the group's symbol and which have circulated widely within the Argentinean imaginary. Another unique aspect of the Madres is their demand for the return of their dead children, as "living ghosts." This clearly impossible demand has served as an important reference point for thinking about the escraches of HIJOS.

that we understand that it's not simply just one more opinion to be agreed with or not.

H: I think this touches on our conviction that we don't just stand for the 30,000 disappeared but that what we represent is much larger. Whoever wants to join can, because there is room for everyone in the escrache. Because of this, I see pamphleteering, for example, as unnecessary. Obviously, however, we prepare a lot, and there is a well thought out discourse.

S: It's that the discourse of HIJOS with the escrache is somehow broader than discourse of HIJOS without the escrache.

H: What's good about the escrache, what's powerful, what's compelling, is that it's a way of saying enough to a lot of things. Above all, to the long years in which we've lived with the laws of impunity and with our anger. I think that in '95 and '96 people reached a breaking point and this could be what provoked the escrache.

H: What you are talking about here also makes it so that when we go to a neighborhood, we almost don't have to explain anything. If we weren't married to what we hate, the escrache wouldn't have, for me, the same force. Because [the slogan begins] "if there is no justice," and we already know that there is no justice, the whole world knows it. It's not just that we say that there's no justice and we make justice with our own hands, but that everyone knows that formal justice is dedicated to protecting people. It's protecting an economic plan; that is, it's really about something else, perhaps some know it and others don't, but these guys are protected by formal justice. And it's not just that we say it, but when we go to an escrache there is a barricade with soldiers and a fence: on one side is the repressor and on the other side is us. The stage is set in such a way that there's nothing to explain. It's something that has become naturalized but there's nothing natural about it. It's a fiction, it's a grand farce that comes apart like a house of cards because it's so poorly built. And it can't be any other way, because the impunity was constructed on passivity, on "yes, it's bad, but what are we going to do?" and not on the will of those of us who remain on the outside. Real Argentineans never chose the laws of Obediencia Debida, the Punto Final, the pardons; they never mobilized for them. Thus, the escrache is like a blow, a blow that strikes and breaks through all this.

H: I think the escrache is of a different stripe; it's a different manner of protesting. In the framework that was mentioned before—between the police, the fences, the repressor, and those of us in the escrache. . . . It's as if the escrache looked at other types of protest and then changed what was a typical march. And in this sense, it's the concept behind it that attracts you, that there are people from the murgas who are there looking for another type of action. When an escrache turns out poorly, it's because it was missing that element that makes people join in, that gives it its strength.

S: Now, something that seems to explain a lot is the idea that the escraches are the result of the kind of questions one asks. That is, the '80s came and went, as did the fraud of democracy, and it seems like that when we went through the difficult '90s, we began to ask ourselves other types of questions. We were not so worried with what our strategy was for taking power, what our strategy was for gaining posts, with how we were going to found a party. The escrache was part of this process. It's a practice of justice that goes beyond waiting. We're no longer waiting for the State to sanction the genocidists or for a future in which the genocidists are in jail. And it seems that this way of looking at things—although perhaps it wasn't a conscious thing—revealed a new type of practice that doesn't worry so much about a far-away tomorrow, that doesn't wait and vote for a good candidate who will resolve the problem of the militarists, the problem of impunity. Instead, the escrache puts the body into action and practices justice, social condemnation, and everything you all put into action now.

H: The justice that the escrache creates exists. But it's necessary to create, little by little, awareness so that there will one day be a consensus for judging the genocidists. We continue to work toward a future in which the genocidists are in prison. And we think that the escrache can serve as a tool for action now, but also that it works for a future . . . for both the escrache and for the truth trials. It's creating a space so that in the future they will actually put the genocidists on trial.[7] One of our goals, among others, is to see all of the genocidists in prison.

H: I don't know if I would agree with you that one day the genocidists will be tried, because we know that they aren't going to do it. Ten, 20, 50 will go, but it'll never happen on a large scale.

S: I want to ask if you think that democracy and justice, as institutions, simply are fine as they are, or if it's the work of HIJOS and other human rights organizations to go further than this type of justice. Because I don't think it's the same

---

[7] *Trans.* In 1999, a series of "truth trials," *juicios por la verdad* as they came to be known, were instituted in Argentina. Because of amnesty laws passed in 1986 and 1987, the hearings sought only to establish the truth about the crimes committed, as there was no possibility either of prosecution or punishment of those involved.

thing. To say that HIJOS is a politics (which isn't a politics of the political parties, but rather a making of justice) is not the same thing as to pretend that a certain institution, the judicial system, for example, works just fine.

H: Of course, but it depends on your perspective on democracy or justice. It depends on what terms you use, if it's a perfect democracy or a democracy in which they try to resolve certain issues and no more. How do you want to approach it?

S: I'd say that there are two levels. One level in which justice is made, for example, by going to escrache a military type, and then another level where one thinks that this turned out well or bad not in and of itself, but because it forced or didn't force a judge to act.

H: You've touched on a point that we've talked about before. The work of HIJOS neither begins nor ends with the escrache and HIJOS doesn't end with just the social condemnation. When we talk about the escrache as consensus we're talking about it in the sense of reacting to what's happening, not just because you live next door to a murderer, but because you can't stand being hungry, because of the schools and everything else. So, I think that talking just about the escrache leaves out the issue you're trying to pose. Personally, I'd like it if the justice system worked, but for this to occur we'd need a social change, a change in the system that realized a different type of justice. I think that the discourse of HIJOS touches on all of this. Because we want the militarists in jail, we want justice, we want to recover the ideals of the disappeared, our friends, and so many others. We do it in our way; we're not a political party; we're not going to run in elections as HIJOS. We do it from the position of a human rights organization. From here, with the limitations that a human rights organization inevitably has, we make our contribution.

S: Here's another critical point to discuss, because we see the escrache as something without limitations, as something that has no limit.[8]

H: I believe that HIJOS is a human rights organization that is different from other such organizations, for a number of reasons. But like all human rights organizations—and this is a personal opinion—it has limits. HIJOS alone won't be able to generate a social change, neither with the escraches nor with 50,000 new activities or practices. That is, HIJOS only, without a political movement, without parties or what have you, with only the things that we have had to invent as a generation won't achieve this. I think that HIJOS is growing not just because of HIJOS, but it's growing because it's in sync with an entire political movement right now that isn't in the parties but that is in the assemblies and social or neighborhood movements. That is, the escraches didn't appear by themselves. Because if we had done it five years before, perhaps it wouldn't have caught on. Here's the point. There has to be a change in order for justice to work and for the militarists to be locked up. The changes we need are many, but the goal is this: I want the militarists to be locked up. For this there needs to be a change? Fine, then we'll build and move forward with the tools that we have

---

[8] *Trans.* The following part of the conversation discusses the idea of "limits" at some length. In part, "limited" means that the escrache does not aspire to be a "universal" program; that is, the escrache's acceptance of its limitations is directly tied to its refusal of politics-as-usual and to its rethinking of what one type of politics without taking power might look like.

at our disposal. Just us, working out of HIJOS, a human rights organization, with all the limitations that it has.

H: To me it seems like we have an idea of the future. If we fixate on the present, then, the escrache becomes the pinnacle of this moment, it's the most that we can hope for. But we're going to continue working. If we think that history ends here, then there's nothing better than the escrache. But we continue thinking, despite the fact we've been disappointed many times, that a transformation is possible in which we will be the protagonists—a transformation greater than the escrache. Our slogan is very clear: if there is no justice, there is escrache. It's because there is no justice, that there is escrache. It's not that the escrache is the best thing that could ever happen to us, it's because in this country there is no justice so we came up with this, which generates a million things, a million new things that are great, that happen in the neighborhoods, that happen in society, that give us the confidence that we can do something to change things. It's good that we have the escrache. But still there is no justice, and justice is what we want. We start from here: if we think of a future, things can be better than a country full of escraches, of hounded criminals. I think things can be better than this. The same force, the same confidence that the escrache gives us, allows us to imagine more ambitious projects perhaps. In this sense, the escrache has limits, because it's not a socialist organization. It's a transformation of a specific area in a neighborhood. Or of a country perhaps. But only at the level of what's going on right now with the genocidists.

The hypotheses for this conversation say "it creates another justice." But it's not that another justice is created and this is the best justice that we can have. Yes, it's the best that we can have in this situation of impunity, but for me the idea of a future continues to exist and to be important.

H: What is created is a new political practice.

S: But why do you think that it's a political practice? On the one hand, you say that the escrache alone won't be able to change things and that it's limited. But to say that the escrache is a new form of politics is to say that the escrache is not just this, it's not something so limited, but rather that it's a new form of politics. It seems to me that it's really important to note this. To say that the escrache is a new form of politics is to say something really positive, really important, and really innovative rather than to say, well, we do this because we can't do anything else, because there are limits, because the parties don't do anything.

What I want to say is this: we believe that the escrache is something really innovative, something very important, and in this conversation we hear you saying: "yes, well we do it because we don't have another option." And, nevertheless, it seems to us that you all are protagonizing something that's really powerful, that is innovative, that affirms things that will be important for another type of politics.[9]

H: I think that it's a political practice that generated— perhaps unconsciously in the sense that it wasn't openly

---

[9] *Trans. Protagonizar* is a verb that is closely associated with the new social movements in Argentina and for which there is no easy translation to English. Generally speaking, *protagonizar* signifies a new, post-1970s sense of agency, wherein people as individuals or groups take control of the formation of their lived reality. Its emphasis is not on the subsuming of the individual into "history," but rather on the potential of the individual to create "situations" (using the vocabulary of Colectivo Situaciones). Because this verb is so critical in describing the sense of agency and relation to history experienced by these movements, and because we believe that there should be more of a two-way street between the vocabularies of English and Spanish, we've decided to translate it as a loan word throughout the text.

stated—a group of people who just got together and started working. This is the important thing. But why did it happen? That's a tougher question. I believe it was historical in part, that at this moment people began looking for new types of social practices. But as for the reason why, I think we can't answer this because still we haven't asked ourselves, well, so why the escrache?

H: Here I agree with you that there isn't a limit, because this practice generated many other political practices. Many others that today one doesn't see or hear about. It gave a push to many young people to do things for themselves, for their neighborhood, for their town, for their union, their school, their college. It put an end to "don't bother with it because everything is rotten; don't bother because it's pointless; don't bother because politics is bad, dirty." In this way, I see it as not having limits. Because today I see those seventeen-year-old kids, and, perhaps when they are twenty-one, they'll overtake HIJOS and everyone else. I think that it's a germ, a seed without limits.

H: I continue to think that it couldn't have played out any other way. The question is why did it take so long to start? That is, nothing else could have happened in these circumstances, in a society where the young people have less and less to lose.

On the other hand, there is a middle position because this justice—our justice—is measured. We don't kill the guy, and we think there is a difference between killing them and escraching them. The escrache was begun from inside existing limitations, from inside what we could create, and we went as far as we could, we chose this path, which can be very radical within certain limits. And it's shaped by our society, a society in which violence is still, as a topic, off-limits. When we go to colleges to talk about the disappeared, everything is fine until we get to the topic of violence and when violence comes up we are trapped by the theory of the two demons, by ourselves, by society. The escrache then is the threshold, it's the limit; that is, it's the most that can be done.

It's not that I'm undervaluing it—for us it's very important. It's what gives us and HIJOS an identity as a political movement: without the escraches we wouldn't be this. We talked about it the other day, that we would be something else if we stopped doing the escraches.

H: I don't know if it's really like that—that it appeared fully formed; rather there were almost four years of working, building the escraches, of transforming them.

H: No, no it doesn't seem to me like it was obvious; what I mean is that this was the most radical level that could be reached. It's more important that the escraches were perfected bit by bit, each time getting better. At first we were very few, there in the Mitre hospital, and for me it was really important that the escraches slowly incorporated other things.[10] But the idea is the same, perfecting them. I just said this a little while ago, it seems to me it's very important that we are not 50 but 500 or 1,000 and that there's a theatre piece, the murga. All this for me is essential, each of the elements of the escrache is essential. But, at the same time, this is our idea of it, and, beyond this idea, there's nothing else. And now there's basically no difference between formal

---

[10] *Trans.* Mitre hospital is located in Buenos Aires. Officials associated with the dictatorship, most importantly Jorge Luis Magnacco, were working there as of 1998.

justice and our justice. Right now, for them, our justice is worse.[11]

S: But the issue is that the escrache is always seen in terms of what it can't do: it can't change the country, it can't change the world, it can't move a million persons, it can't kill all the bad guys nor all the genocidists, it can't do a lot of things. But it's precisely on this type of thinking, a thinking of what can't be done, that the political parties of every society are founded. But the escraches differentiate themselves because there are things that they can do. And unlike a thousand talking heads, the escrache can do certain things. And if one judges it only on what it can't do, this seems incredibly unjust. It's more than this. A traditional left militant might say to HIJOS: "Well, what you do is fine, but look, will you take power? Will you change society? It lacks politics." Now, if we set ourselves to look at who today is doing something, what acts really have effects, it seems to me that the escraches are much better than the majority of things being done. It looks really quite strong.

H: Well, I think, speaking optimistically, that the collective identity of HIJOS was, in some way, created via a dialogue with society. And that during these years HIJOS, albeit unconsciously, learned to read the social and to generate a new political practice that people had sympathy with. I think that HIJOS created this, but that it's also growing as both society and HIJOS are changing. There is a maturing process, and the escrache is a part of this.

---

[11] *Trans.* This refers to the fact that being "out-ed" in their neighborhood is a worse punishment than going to jail for many of the genocidists. This is what the social condemnation amounts to.

H: On the topic of the escraches as taken up by other groups, I think that sometimes it's okay and sometimes not. A lot of times there is opportunism, which the hypotheses for this discussion noted. An opportunism that is really annoying, like when the Menemist Youth escrached Shuberof, because they're assholes.[12] They distorted the escrache; they turned it into shit; they ruined it. Or when, for example, the parties of the left do one—well they aren't assholes but there is definitely a great deal of opportunism. Because the escrache is a tool, and, like all tools, if you misuse it, in an instant it loses its power.

S: Now, to me, it seems that there's something with the escrache that goes beyond a certain group using it, and it's when the escrache becomes a tool of negotiation for obtaining a budget, a salary, or whatever else. Then it loses something.

H: I think that what's distorted is the form of the escrache, the form that we give it. In this sense, yes it's a new form of making politics, which is accompanied by a new aesthetic form of political participation. We break with the

---

[12] *Trans.* It's important to note that only HIJOS goes into the neighborhoods, flyering etc. and that's why all "appropriations" of the escrache as a form by other groups fail (as is being discussed here). The point is that the escrache is something more complicated than just having some performance art and throwing paint at a building. Oscar Shuberof was the director of the University of Buenos Aires during the presidency of Menem and fought against many of Menem's neoliberal programs. However, in the end, Shuberof opened the university to privatization and moved to strengthen ties between education and business. As such, he is a reviled figure among past and present student groups. The Menemist Youth was a political youth organization (similar to something like the Young Republicans) which supported President Menem.

traditional protest march, because the idea of an artistic alternative appeared, of allowing theatre groups, murga groups, to participate. And they are all groups that have a certain distance from the institutions. In this sense, then, it's also a new form of joining art, politics, and memory. And this is what the other escraches lose, the aesthetic part. But the political part depends on who does it.

S: But there's another reason why it's a new form of politics and why it's different from a march. And it's that the march, in the end, asks for something. That is, it tries to touch a nerve so that some part of the institutional system decides to be in favor of what the march asks for. And that's fine. But the escrache doesn't ask for anything, because, as you said earlier, justice isn't going to happen; we know that. The escrache, then, is an alternative. No matter how much creating formal justice is a goal, the escrache will take on another meaning, because we know that having thousands of marches isn't going to bring about justice. I think that the central issue here is that the escraches are a new form of making justice, and here is the reason why—returning to the beginning—it goes beyond consensus. I think that if we continue talking about this we will begin to understand why the escrache is a new form of making politics.

It has to do with the future: the escrache can't be seen as depending on the future. On the contrary, the future, will depend on what happens with the escrache and with similar political practices, even though they won't have the same form but a similar sense. And these practices will spread throughout all of society, throughout all of the ideas that constitute it.

A similar example is the Landless Workers Movement of Brazil which for years has been asking for agrarian reform and which will continue to do so. At some point, they'll give it to them or not, but they are already taking the land and beginning to live in another manner.

In this, I see something fundamental. Before, you said that the escrache doesn't change society, that the escrache changes the idea of justice that exists in society, but not ALL of society. Fine, the escrache doesn't have to give itself the task of changing all of society, even though HIJOS might want this, because there are many other experiences that exist, and these will create in other areas practices with the same meaning as the escrache. But, because of this, what has to be asked is why the escrache is an example, why it's a new form that implies a new politics. If we look at it in this way, I think the escrache doesn't have any limits. If not, we run the risk of falling into the classical schema of politics, where the social is limited because it doesn't touch or transform politics as a whole. This schema says that the social is divided into sectors and that, thus, politics has to come and take up different ideas, different struggles, education, neighborhoods, the escrache, etc, and resolve them via politics, from power. The truth is that after FrePaSO, for us at least, it's crystal clear that this doesn't work.[13] This is a clear, recent example of how there is a logic in classical politics, in the politics of consensus, of the relations of power in society, of the State, that makes it so people, who end up thinking of politics as a set of goals to be achieved, really transform very little. But, on the other hand, we have a guy who doesn't think like this but who begins work-

---

[13] *Trans.* The Frente País Solidario is a political party formed in the 1990s, which became the primary opposition to the presidency of Menem. When they took second place in the elections of 1995, this broke the traditional bipartisan structure of the Argentinean political system. In 1999, they won the presidential elections with Eduardo Duhalde as their candidate, but his term was cut short by the popular insurrection of December 19 and 20, 2001.

ing on something like the escrache. Someone, who doesn't wait for a court to hand down a favorable judgment, but who instead does an escrache in order to create justice in Argentina, in order to change the very idea of justice.

S: It's like when Chiapas happened and the whole world said: "Chiapas, a singular event. It's good, but too bad that it's only an example, nothing more." When, in fact, there are hundreds of things that are happening with a similar logic, which we could look toward instead of looking at Chiapas and saying "look at the limits of Chiapas." To want to look for the limitations of Chiapas is to look at it from the position of power, in an incredible way. Because they can't be judged by their inability to transform the planet. It's absurd. In fact, they don't pretend to. Therefore, when something appears that begins to transform, there's always a discourse that says, "Well, fine, you changed this, but what about the rest?" Right now, the problem is that everyone who wants to change things globally always tells us that nothing can be changed.

Therefore, what we see is that everywhere phenomena begin to appear whose point in common is to change certain ideas, to do really powerful things, of which there are two possible readings. The first condemns them because they can't change the world. For example, "Why do an escrache? Does it give us justice? Change the country? Expropriate the means of production? No? Well, then no to the escraches. Thus, the party."

But if it's not like this, our concern is how one begins to look at these experiences as just the opposite: not for what they can't do, but for everything they can do in a time in which it was said that nothing more could be done. In a time, then, in which nothing can be done, many experiences, all very different, appear. On the surface, Chiapas and the escrache don't have anything to do with each other, but, on a deeper level, it appears that yes they do. And it has to do more than with just HIJOS and the peasant-farmers of Chiapas. You say that the escrache appeared, that you had to wait a long time, and then Chiapas happened, although they had to wait a longer time. No one believes that these things are the product of some mind that planned them; instead they just appear. And there are many more of these experiences, perhaps smaller, going on right now.

H: At one time we talked a lot about one of our key ideas: "justice and punishment." But what judgment and what punishment? Who hands down this justice? We don't believe in established justice because it has shown us that it's unaccountable. We considered, then, the escrache as a mode of changing justice. At some point, we discussed if the escrache was popular justice. I think that we decided that there is another type of justice, in which people from the neighborhoods create another justice, one that is created amongst ourselves, between neighbors, between HIJOS, between the murgas and those that come and denounce these guys who our current justice has left free. Thus, we tried and we said: yes it can be done, justice can be changed by everyone, amongst everyone.

H: To change it no; rather to create another justice. That's something different.

H: We also talked about the idea of prisons. Some said that prisons are not forms of justice. The escrache, then, is a way of beginning to raise this issue.

H: I think that we never undertook an analysis of the escrache like you all are doing. We never sat down and seriously posed these questions to ourselves. And it's not that we don't have a political analysis because yes we do, but rather that we didn't draw out all the possibilities. Thus, looking at it from the inside, perhaps we felt that the possibilities for doing certain things had limits.

S: It's not a problem of levels of analysis, because in the end you all had a political discourse that made the escraches and that worked very well. We have another concern that isn't more important but just different, and it's seeing if the escraches are just the escraches or if they are a part of something larger, which is just beginning to be seen. Something like a stance common to multiple struggles, struggles which are not subordinated to any political party and which will not be in the future. Struggles which begin looking for something different, which begin searching without knowing exactly for what.

H: Well, I think that it's what someone said before, that one looks for a popular justice and that this goes beyond formal justice. In this sense, it's certain that the escrache doesn't have limitations. Where it has limits is as a specific political practice; in perhaps 10 years the practice will be totally different and it will have another name—but with this same idea, with this same truth. Because I identify myself with a group who has a certain political consciousness, who looked for this specific activity, but who, over time, via a process of maturing, is going to arrive at another type of practice. The group, the idea, is this: it's the desire to create a parallel justice, a popular power. In this sense, yes, there are no limits. But, here, the limit would be thinking about how we are moving forward. At the last Congress of HIJOS, for example, we were talking about the reconstruction of the social fabric and this has a lot to do with the escraches as well.

H: I'm still stuck on what someone said earlier, about how the escrache changed something in the kids, that it pushed them to do something about their own problems. In this sense, it seems to me that the escrache also contrasts with the politics of the specialists, technicians, professionals. That is, you can go to an escrache just as you are, you don't need a doctorate from Harvard, and because you don't have to go and talk on TV, you can come in shorts, however you like. Any person can make politics, they only have to make the decision, be committed and get together with other people. It seems that this is what was transformed in these kids, because for many youth, politics is synonymous with the party, with advertising and billboards.

And this really worked against us, especially in the beginning, when people would say to us, "But I thought that the escraches were part of party X." Why? "Because I've seen all those posters over there." This happened frequently.

For many people, the escrache was what made them see that politics isn't so bad, and they got closer and stayed closer to it. This to me seems very, very important, because it went completely against current thinking, and we understood that. So, this shift is something powerful that the escrache created.

Concerning what you all said about the slogan, "If there is no justice, there is escrache," that it asks for nothing, at one point it reminded me of the "Living Ghost," which also doesn't ask for anything. The first time I went to the Plaza de Mayo and saw the women there, I didn't understand anything. It was like 5 years ago. I talked with the Madres, and I thought they were crazy, I didn't understand. Because I went there, and I wasn't waiting for the "living ghost" of my wife and I wondered what are these people doing? But the escrache is a little like this: to ask for the impossible.

S: Yes, they seem really similar to me as well. Many people who see what you all say about "there could be justice," are going to dismiss you no matter what. But in reality, it seems to me that this phrase of the Madres, or this phrase of yours, provides a ground for something that is very difficult to create. It's the fact that you all don't need to say "come to the escrache so that they'll increase your salary; come to the escrache so that they'll increase your retirement." You don't have to sign up the badly off, but instead you say something that is obvious and that doesn't directly benefit yourselves: you're posing a question of universal justice here, very clearly. Because of this, the whole world can come without having to demand something. I don't need, if I was a student, to say, "Well, what does HIJOS think about trade barriers?" Nor would it occur to me to think that that was important. With the Madres this also happened, because no one was going to ask them, before helping them, what they thought of this, that, or the other, because it was clear, from the beginning, that they weren't asking for anything for themselves. They were doing something incredibly universal without having to sign up other groups. And here the idea of consensus returns, of not having to negotiate: we want them to return our children, who everyone knows are dead. Now, what that phrase and that scarf achieved was incredible.

Neither the escraches, nor phrases like these are really credible, because no one thinks—not to disillusion you all—that there will be justice in Argentina for the militarists. But the idea is that no one goes to the escraches because they think there will be justice, but because justice is there, there in the escraches. And this brings out a lot of people, without the necessity of knowing if it's "working," if some judge will feel touched by it, if some political party. . . . It brings out people who don't care what HIJOS thinks about their particular social conditions.

H: In any case, with all this, HIJOS is raising two issues. One is the escrache and the other is participating in certain juridical possibilities that exist, that are concrete. Because for us to put away two or three more is not nothing, it's something. But this is not our cause.

H: This perhaps can appear contradictory, but the idea is to create a disturbance on every level, to do the most that can be done in every area.

S: Of course, and it's not contradictory in any way. But what is the difference between a human rights lawyer working to imprison those who they can, doing the possible, and the escraches, which I think go beyond this? Human rights organizations always have existed, now there is Garzon and that's great.[14] We all want them to be in jail but the escrache lays out a different scenario.

I wanted to pose a different question to you all, and I don't know if it will be very involved. What I want to ask about is this: HIJOS with the escrache seems to think of the past in a completely different way than it has previously been thought. Because the past is usually discussed as something that's already occurred, that is now history, something that some people will still want to talk about because they don't want to look ahead. HIJOS makes the past live again, here, in the present, as something that happens in the now. The escrache makes the past present, it makes that soldier there and you all here a part of the present. What do you

---

[14] *Trans.* Baltasar Garzón, the Spanish judge responsible for investigating and bringing to trial, via extradition, many members of the Argentinean dictatorship. His work during the late 1990s re-opened the possibility of legal redress for crimes committed during the dictatorship.

think about this? Because this is another very important issue and a very generationally marked one.

H: I see it as very related to the idea of dismantling the repressive apparatus as well. The repressors of yesterday are the same as those of today. There are a huge number of cases, beginning with the solider from Cutral Có who killed Teresa Rodríguez and who also was a repressor in Tucumán in the '70s.[15] In this sense as well, we make the past present. They are here, and they continue, continue robbing, continue killing. Some are businessmen who got rich during the dictatorship, like Blaquier.[16] In this sense, the militarists who are poorly off are few. The majority are inside the system, working for the intelligence services. Like this, then, the past is present.

On the other hand, I'm in agreement with what you say, because the truth is that the majority of us are sick and tired of them telling us, "Enough with the past; why don't you think about the present." It's a discourse that they use to avoid you. Exactly because of this, one job of the escrache is to place everything out in the open and say: "This is how it is." It's not finished, you or I could meet this guy on the street. And that's a strong argument against those who say that we are stuck in the past.

---

[15] *Trans.* In April of 1998, Teresa Rodríguez, a mother of three, was shot dead in the town of Cutral Có, Neuquén Province, during clashes between demonstrators and members of the police. A province of Argentina, famous for its poverty and for its agricultural production, which was also the site of some of the most brutal repression seen during the dictatorship, frequently in order to protect the interests of international corporations.

[16] *Trans.* Argentinean banker.

A TEXT FOR THE ESCRACHE OF WEBER

a document of HIJOS

TODAY WE ARE in front of the house of another torturer: Ernesto Enrique Frimon Weber, Subcommisioner of the Federal Police of Argentina who acted as a repressor during the military dictatorship in the clandestine extermination center operated out of the Escuela de Mecanica de la Armada (E.S.M.A.).

He was a torturer and a kidnapper and, as a member of the Logistic Division of Work Group 3.3.2, responsible for the kidnapping of more than 3,500 people. He acted under the pseudonym 220, a nickname given to him in recognition of his skill with a cattle prod.

Free under the Punto Final law, he was then accused, in an international indictment issued by Spanish judge Baltasar Garzón, of the crimes of genocide and state terrorism. He lives at Virgilio 1245, Apartment 3, his phone number is 4567-2112.

Four years have already passed since our first escrache in December of 1996. In these four years, the escrache has become a new tool for struggle. The escrache has been and is a way to transform memory into action, a new way of denouncing impunity. It is way of demonstrating that impunity is not an abstract noun. Rather, impunity is a very concrete term: impunity is Emilio Eduardo Massera supposedly detained in his mansion on Avenue Libertador; it's Miguel Etchecolatz walking through the Plazas of Córdoba and Jean Jaurés; it's José Alfredo Martínez de Hoz editorializing from "the city"[1] about the direction of the world's economy; it's Julián the Turk having coffee at a bar on Congreso; it's Fernando Peyón protected by the police of District 39 in Villa Urquiza (who showed no remorse after they burnt the arm of one of the Plaza de Mayo mothers); it's Norberto Bianco working in his clinic in San Miguel under the permission granted by Aldo Rico; it's Nelly Arrieta de Blaquier, who presides over the Asociación de Amigos del Museo de Bellas Artes.

Impunity lives on in each of these people: repressors, torturers, appropriators,[2] genocidists, authors of the extermination of millions of militants who fought against privilege and inequality. This same inequality is today the supreme law of the Argentinean republic. Because of this, the escrache has been and continues to be a blow for justice. A justice based in the certainty that real justice will not fall from the treetops of power like a rotten fruit. A justice that understands that when a crime is organized from within the state, it's society that must identify the criminals, judge them, sentence them, persecute them, and pursue them even into their dreams. A justice of the people who haven't forgotten or forgiven the terrorism of the State, the con-

---

[1] Trans. The downtown financial district of Buenos Aires.

[2] *Trans.* "Appropriation" refers to the practice, instituted under the dictatorship, of illegally giving children born either while their mothers were imprisoned or taken from them while imprisoned, to the families and friends of military personnel.

centration camps, the torture, the "flights of death,"[3] the "appropriated" children, though some continue to talk of reconciliation. Although some are still waiting for a day when suddenly we'll wake up and society will be reconciled with its executioners, the very same executioners who never paid for their crimes and who today are engaged in the same activities, repressing people or working for the SIDE of the banker Santibañes.[4]

The reconciliation offered to us by the dominant classes, in spite of their differing versions (De la Rúa, Brinzoni, the church)[5], is just a formula that implies FORGETTING and SILENCE without PUNISHMENT. We call that impunity. That is why we don't want to be reconciled with something that we never shared. We don't want to be reconciled with the genocidists nor with those who want to save them from the fire of social condemnation. Their tarnished names burn in that fire. In that fire, there is no forgetting and no forgiveness.

The escrache, then, is our most sincere response to the much-discussed reconciliation. Today we are in front of the house of the repressor W to respond to this offer of reconciliation made to us by the powers-that-be. Our answer is that W is free, that W tortured, kidnapped, murdered, stole, and was left free. Our answer is that there are thousands like him walking happily through the streets of

---

[3] *Trans.* The "vuelos de la muerte" was a tactic used by the state to "disappear" people, where they were pushed while still alive from planes into the Rio de la Plata or into the Atlantic Ocean.

[4] *Trans.* The Secretaría de Inteligencia del Estado (SIDE) is the most important intelligence service of the Argentinean government. The SIDE was responsible for much of the state terrorism during the dictatorship. Fernando de Santibáñes was the head of the SIDE during the government of Fernando de la Rúa (1999–2001).

[5] *Trans.* The dominant classes being the government (De la Rúa), the bankers (Brinzoni), and the church.

our country. Our answer is that we're not going to stay at home crying for our fallen, that we'll go to the streets, that we'll take back public space, that sooner or later it's them who won't be able to leave their houses. Already there are many who can't leave Argentina because there are other countries who are willing to pursue them into whatever corner of the world they decide to hide in. Olivera and Cavallo have already found this out.[6]

For the genocidists like W, Argentina is both a prison and a refuge. The territory in which they committed their crimes has become the only place on the planet where they enjoy relative peace. Here they don't need to answer to institutional justice; in fact, the government considers them to be normal citizens.

But not even the most naïve of the genocidists could believe that the protection given to them by Menem and upheld by the government of De la Rúa is everything. Official impunity cannot free them from social condemnation. Julian the Turk knows this and well. Weber will probably begin to accept this tomorrow when he steps outside and notices that many recognize him, that many know who he is, that many know what he tried to hide for so long. And, in the eyes of the neighborhood, he will once again be the torturer he has never ceased to be.

Because of all this, the escrache doesn't have an expiration date. Because it has become a practice that doesn't depend on who is warming the seats in the Casa Rosada.[7] Because it doesn't matter if some TV station comes, or

---

[6] *Trans.* Jorge Olivera Rovere is a former military leader who was detained in Italy on the order of a French judge for the disappearance of a Franco-Argentinean woman. Ricardo Miguel Cavallo was detained in Mexico on an international warrant issued by Spanish judge Baltasar Garzón.

[7] *Trans.* The Argentinean "White House."

doesn't come, to cover it for the nightly news. Because it isn't bothered by the most ridiculous editorials in *La Nación*, whose editorials recently praised Videla and that now proclaim "the importance of living in a democracy." Because it has its own life outside the society of the spectacle. This life, born of the meeting where the escrache was first imagined, which grew stronger with the work in the neighborhoods and which has fed a dialogue and debate with those neighbors who refused to live any longer with a murderer. Moreover, their desire wasn't exhausted by this process (rather the opposite). Tomorrow, the shop owner won't sell to him; the taxi-driver won't pick him up; the baker will choose not to wait on him; the paperboy will refuse to deliver the newspaper. And the following day the struggle will multiply.

For all of this, we continue to work. We continue to carry the faces of the disappeared for all to see in each mobilization, because we haven't forgotten their struggle for a country without exclusion, because we haven't forgotten their commitment to transformation, because we carry with us their dreams and their example. Because we will not forget that they fought for a country for everyone. Because we know that they were "disappeared," were locked up, murdered, and forced into exile to consolidate a group's vision of this country. A country where what is needed in the slums is found in excess in the private neighborhoods and weekend homes in the country, where many have very little and where a few take home everything, where government officials turn politics into a synonym for bribery and they "adjust" us in order to pay the IMF.

For all of this and because we know that we are many, those who want another country, we continue to struggle, with humility, hope, and conviction. Without sectarianism, without leaders who hide amongst their miseries the salvation for the entire universe, without authoritarianism, and without pause.

IF THERE IS NO JUSTICE THERE IS ESCRACHE

ANOTHER GOVERNMENT, THE SAME IMPUNITY

WE RECLAIM THE STRUGGLE OF OUR FATHERS AND MOTHERS

WE WILL NOT FORGET

WE WILL NOT FORGIVE

WE WILL NOT BE RECONCILED

12 HYPOTHESES/QUESTIONS CONCERNING THE ESCRACHES

Colectivo Situaciones

1

THE ESCRACHE IS a hypothesis-in-practice that was launched by the group HIJOS halfway through the last decade. This hypothesis has not only persisted; it has taken root and branched out. Today's escraches, more than yesterday's, plunge into the community and work with the residents of that community. They have developed as well an "un-selfishness," a "for everyone," that has been lost in contemporary political activity.

2

"BECAUSE THERE IS no justice," there is the escrache. This negative motivation opens a space not for lament, but rather for self-affirmation, for the symbolic and political production of justice based in social condemnation. In this way, the escrache involves exercising the capacity to create.

The escrache, however, is not static. In fact, its very existence depends on its capacity to self-develop.[1] But in order
to do so, it must combat the agents of its neutralization:
virtualization, imitation, media saturation, and the tran-
quilizing effects of success. The escrache valorizes autonomy
in so far as it allows one to abandon acting via opposition.
Its independence with respect to the other—the enemy,
the system—converts the escrache into an instrument of
self-affirmation, giving it permanent capacity for self-
production and for thinking for itself. The escrache then
corrects and re-verifies itself on a case-by-case basis. As
such, the escrache, since its inception, has gone through
a series of phases: from the first actions in the center of
the city to the actions in the outlying neighborhoods and
suburbs of the capital; from its original position—relatively
naïve—with respect to the media and to militancy to its
unfolding in the public spaces of daily life; from its original
and fleeting vision to a set of ideas developed and worked
on for many months in conjunction with various local
organizations.

---

[1] *Trans.* Although a bit awkward in English, we've decided (here
and throughout the remainder of the text) to literally translate
the Spanish *autoafirmación*, as well as similar terms such as *au-
todesarrollo* or *autoproducción*, by maintaining the prefix "self-";
thus yielding "self-affirmation," "self-development," "self-pro-
duction," etc. We've done so in order to highlight two critical
aspects of Colectivo Situaciones' interpretation of the escrache,
which are dependent on the literal rendering of this prefix. First,
that the escrache produces itself and its context and, second,
that it's a "hypothesis-in-practice," which means that it corrects
and adjusts itself as it proceeds, that it is not a universal method
or a strategy.

3

THE ESCRACHE CANNOT be thought of via dichotomies such as "inside/outside" or "exterior/interior." A better starting point would be the escrache's "tranversality."[2] The escrache does not come from the "outside," nor does it simply exist in the neighborhood. Rather, the escrache is produced in an encounter during which something in common emerges between the Mesa de Escrache Popular,[3] the community, and the other participants. This *something in common* emerges from certain shared historical circumstances and the hypothesis-in-practice that is the escrache.

The escrache's lack of respect for established boundaries and borders demonstrates the potential of its thinking; its capacity to create a space that can incorporate people who lack any connection to politics.

---

[2] *Trans.* A term first developed by Guattari within the context of his psychoanalytic practice at La Borde, and elaborated on by Deleuze and Guattari where they speak of transversal practices as methods of de-territorialization. Generally speaking, transversality concerns the opening up of logics and hierarchies and the creation of new "collective assemblages" or group, social, and/or individual relations. Within a more directly political context, Guattari deployed transversality as a way of critiquing the institutionality of political organizations (especially "the party"). Another important valance of the term that can be heard here is the idea, in Guattari, that transversality can produce new types of collective subjectivity that open up both the group and the individual.

[3] *Trans.* The Mesa de Escrache is a group composed of a wider range of persons and collectives than HIJOS (although it includes members of HIJOS) that during 2000–2001 began to take on a more prominent role in the organizing and operation of the escraches.

4

Has the escrache been *generalized*?[4] This is a difficult question to answer.

Without a doubt its influence has increased and it has been appropriated by the neighborhood assemblies.

However, in what sense can this be considered a "generalization"? We need to explain in what sense we can speak of a "generalization of the escrache."

We propose thinking about this problem as such:

a) An escrache becomes generalized when it can be said that it "does not have an author"—when the escrache thinks itself, uniting a variety of different individuals and social groups with its logic, which is itself subject to on-going verification.

b) When its sense and roots are found in diverse situations (transversality) and when it is not the victim of mere copy or imitation.

c) When it is propagated, by whatever means possible, through alternative circuits of social production.

This generalization, understood as above, from the escrache's situation, implies methods of diffusion that avoid the pitfalls of serialization, fetishization, spectacle, banal modelization, easy imitation, instrumentalization, and purely media-based circulation.

But these clues are, in reality, questions. In what sense, can we speak of a "generalization" of the escrache?

---

[4] *Trans.* The meaning of "generalize" that we're calling upon here is "to spread throughout the body and become systemic" where, in this case, the body would be Argentinean society. The Spanish *generalizar* also carries another sense of generalize that we'd like the reader to hear, namely, "to give a general form to." In this case, something close to, but less pejorative than, the English "to popularize."

5

IF THE DICTATORSHIP opened the path to neoliberalism, the escrache declares that this was because the repression fragmented the social body. The escrache, then, produces *social bonds in order to counteract their on-going and systematic destruction.*

In this way, the escrache can be thought of as part of the emergence of a new social protagonism and of alternative networks of social actors who are looking to shed the rule of capital and the state-mafia.

For us, it is obvious that the escrache produces its own context. It doesn't enter the world-as-such without changing it. On the contrary, it creates possible, alternative forms of being in the world. It creates something that was not there before. It produces concrete forms of political intervention. It energizes and speaks to other instances of the new social protagonism. The escrache is a radically singular occurrence, at the same time that it is a sign of a moment that is generating a new radicalism.

The escrache, as a situational hypothesis-in-practice, self-corrects, subjecting itself to on-going changes and verifications. But the escrache is not the only possible hypothesis nor is it a privileged one. Because "it is" not only what it is, but it is also that which catalyzes, which expresses, which emerges from the context that it produces.

In this sense, the days of December 19th and 20th have also been produced by the escrache.

6

AND THIS IS another way of thinking about the "generalization" of the escrache.

After December 19th and 20th of 2001, people's understanding of their situation has been transformed. It is now widely recognized that in Argentina there are social struggles and these concrete experiences of resistance are of interest.

What, then, is the connection between the Mesa de Escrache and the neighborhood assemblies?

How can we understand the appropriation of the escraches by the assemblies?

In this context, what does the singularity of the escraches of HIJOS consist of? Does this singularity exist?

7

THE JOURNEY OF the "hijos" ("children") from a group of individuals who had been victims of the same injustice to HIJOS, a collective with the capacity to create, among other things, the escrache, has been a journey towards multiplicity. A journey in which seizing the initiative and speaking out are revealed as the sources of creation.

In this sense, the escrache is part of this passage from suffering and self-identification as "victims" to an active and productive subjectivity. It is the passage from the imposition of a name to the ability to construct a subjectivity based in this imposition.

Thus, the escrache calls into question this "given" identity, that of victims. For HIJOS, it is not just a matter of being "marked" by the same event; instead, they take this experience and re-signify it and turn it into an active and creative principle that goes beyond the "mark" imposed by the terrorism of the State. *Because of this, the escrache ceases to be solely an activity of HIJOS and becomes a truly autonomous practice, autonomous even from its creators. Thus, with the invention of the escrache, "we all can be hijos."*

These terms become de-centered. The escrache is no longer done because one is a "hijo" or a part of HIJOS, rather a new subject emerges when all the dimensions and implications of the escrache are experienced. No single person oversees or constructs the escrache, rather all who participate are taken up by its power. The goal now is to rise to the challenge of the escrache.

In this sense, identity is enriched when it is lived as part of an unfolding practice, instead of being seen as a predetermined set of possibilities. Perhaps here, the experience of HIJOS reveals a generational dimension to the present struggles. "Generational" in the sense of a set of common questions, perhaps the same ones as always, but formulated anew in the heat of these experiences.

8

THE ESCRACHE SHOULD not be measured by its size. Its value exceeds both measurement and scale. Its relation to quantity is not quantitative.

Revolutionary politics, almost always, has taken the form of a "willing majority." Most often, radical critique, as well as the desire to transform and liberate, must be negotiated within a complex web of existing power and relations of force, and it often loses its edge with the need to create alliances and to construct a totalizing hegemony. However, taking refuge in a speculative and purely negative critique is not an alternative.

The escrache is a practical example of a minoritarian ethics of justice that has remained un-negotiable in its most profound sense. It acquires its true radicalism and power when it manages to create an acting collective body. This minority, then, is not an elite. It is not an issue of there being a majority or a minority, but rather of the abandoning of a quantitative measure for a situational one.

The escrache wants to spread, to reach as many people as it possibly can, but this growth is qualitative. To grow is to verify, to develop, to intensify the work. This is not to say that numbers don't matter, but rather that, here, they are at the service of the process and the product.

The escrache, as a product, cannot be separated from the process that produces it. And that is its best weapon against virtualization. Here, we can see its multiplicity unfolds across various levels: on the one hand, abandoning the one-dimensionality that the mass media condemns it to and, on the other, acquiring new meanings beyond pure denunciation.

The escrache, then, disseminates itself without having to worry about the "accumulation" or "administration" of those who participate in it.

Its street and community-oriented dynamic arrives, works, and leaves, but the escrache remains.

The escrache unfolds horizontally and thus mixes with other forms of struggle.

9

THE "VIOLENCE" OF the escraches has been singled out and roundly denounced both in the media and by politicians.[5] This denunciation is naïve, as it fails to grasp the extent to which the escraches are implicated in the production of contemporary radical subjectivity.

To sustain and unfold this subjectivity is doubly difficult, since the existing forms of political thought must be fought off: on the one hand, the subjectivity of "the seventies" and, on the other, the "human rights" subjectivity.

---

[5] *Trans.* In this discussion of violence, Situaciones are referring to the right-wing, government, and media attempts to label the escrache as a violent or "fascist" practice. The escraches are clearly nonviolent actions. Thus, the word "violence" here in quotes is an ironic reference to these attempts to suppress the escrache by slander.

Thus, those who reclaim the "revolutionary" tradition attempt to reproduce the experience of the seventies and, as a consequence, see violence as a fundamental part of a political strategy of taking power and as the only way to realize justice. On the other side are those who work with the subjectivity inherited from the post-dictatorship era: a "democratic" subjectivity that subordinates the existential demands of justice to relations of power and, thus, condemns violence in abstract terms.

But, now, we are not in a dictatorship of the state but rather of the market. Furthermore, we are no longer in the "post-dictatorship" era, rather we are in the post-democracy era, a moment distinguished by market domination. A contemporary subversive subjectivity is one that manages to think and to unfold practices from within this new situation. Since the hegemony of the market produces the dispersion, fragmentation, and virtualization of practices, a contemporary radical subjectivity cannot be formed without assuming this condition as a starting point. The risks run by this subjectivity are two-fold: becoming entangled in a pure present without memory or living a life based only in nostalgia.

The escrache, then, is located in a different place; it is an investigation, intervention, and experiment. The violence implied in the escrache is incomprehensible without taking into consideration the conditions of those who participate in the escrache's investigation.

Unarmed and uninterested in power, the escraches are not acts of resentment, even though resentment remains. Contrary to the frequent public comparisons that have been made (by both the right and the left) between the escrache and the street activities of fascists, the escrache does not suppress any reality, it does not eliminate lives, it is not just a denouncement, it does not repress, it does not impoverish. Instead, it aggregates, it unites, and it creates. It does not mutilate reality, rather it multiplies it.

10

THE ESCRACHE IS a practice that converts sadness and impotence (and the desire for vengeance) into active and productive principles for justice and commitment. It is not an act of vengeance, even though this is also present in it.

The escrache is undertaken in those places that the representative justice of the state has deserted. It is a practice of self-affirmation created to confront a brutal act of judicial marginalization *and is not inscribed in a frustrated desire for inclusion but in its opposite: a desire for justice that persists in spite of this frustration.*

The disappeared (those who survived and those who did not) have been excluded from all justice in the name of justice itself. Family members, friends, and compatriots of the disappeared are completely justified in claiming that they have been irreparably damaged. However, the matter does not end here; instead, at this point, a possibility, an alternative to frustration, reveals itself. An alternative runs from the Madres of the Plaza de Mayo to HIJOS, from the slogan of "living ghosts" to the escraches. The alternative is the refusal of people who have been excluded or disappeared to remain silent and to affirm an active subjectivity in response to this exclusion. The exclusion, once seen from this perspective, can then be used to produce other practices, different from those that have been institutionalized, which can then be deployed as instruments of justice.

11

THE ESCRACHE OF HIJOS is a virtuous exercise of history: a subtle conjunction of past, present, and future dimensions. A fold.[6]

The memory called forth by the escrache is not that of pure recall, but one that is capable of producing powerful images out of the present situation. It does not operate as a finished account from the end of history, but as a useful political resource.

History is assumed from the rupture: a *historic* rupture of history itself. An updating of eternal possibilities in new and open forms.

In the escrache, we hear the demands of an era as heard by those who will answer them.

12

BETWEEN THE FRAGMENTATION caused by market capitalism and the centralization promoted by the politics of "short cuts," a middle ground exists. The search for this middle ground is based in encounter and exchange. It is a search, a process without end whose force is the intensity of situational experience. And this quality of searching is the shared desire that links the escrache with so many other contemporary experiences.

---

[6] *Trans.* This is an explicit reference to Paolo Virno's usage of the term as set forth in his "Virtuosity and Revolution." The article can be found at the 16 Beaver Street website: www.16beavergroup. org/mtarchive/archives/000941.php

COLECTIVO SITUACIONES IN CONVERSATION WITH THE MESA DE ESCRACHE POPULAR

1. DISPLACEMENTS

MESA DE ESCRACHE: I'd like to discuss the hypothesis that begins "there is escrache because there is no justice." I'd say that yes there is justice, a justice of the system, an *institutional* justice. But what we do is construct *another* justice, which we understand in a very different way, another idea, another practice, something that's constructed in the neighborhoods. A justice that is *social condemnation*. Because of this, I think that with or without justice, there is still *escrache*.

M: However, we came to this conclusion only after a long process of growing, growing up as it were. In reality, according to an early document of HIJOS, the escrache came about *because there is no* justice. Afterwards, we realized that even if "there is justice," there will still be escrache.

M: This has been a subject for debate from the very start of HIJOS. I think that it's more important to continue practicing a *popular* justice than to continue demanding "justice and punishment."[1] That is, I think that the escrache goes beyond "justice and punishment." I think we have to consider changing the slogan to say that because there is justice, which couldn't be more inept and dysfunctional, there is escrache.

M: I'm not in complete agreement with this. Because it's true that there is a corrupt and inept justice, but I don't believe that it's necessary to legitimate this justice. For me, this justice doesn't exist; thus, I'm not going to say "there's justice."

M: Perhaps it's necessary to differentiate between "the just" and "justice." Because on the one hand, there is an institution that dispenses *(in)justice*, and, on the other, there are *acts* of justice that are separate from this order, that have nothing to do with justice, but that are instead social condemnation. From this perspective, our understanding of the escrache changes, because by thinking of justice as social condemnation the escrache has to be related to other social actors and in a new way. If the escrache has as an end "justice and punishment," then it's related to the media in a manner that your hypotheses call "naïve," but I don't think that's what's happening. Because what we want is to *move* people. If the escrache is just a way to "judge and punish," then the media works effectively, rapidly, and reaches millions. But when there is a *displacement* and when one doesn't just ask them for justice and punishment, now we're in the realm of social condemnation . . . it's not about

---

[1] *Trans.* "Justice and punishment" is another early slogan of HIJOS. The Argentinean art collective Grupo Arte Callejero incorporated it into one of the signs they designed to be hung or pasted along the route of the escrache, and it has since become an iconic symbol of the escrache.

asking anyone for anything nor attacking the institutions. Instead the escrache moves to the neighborhood and the relation with the media becomes secondary. Now we connect with the neighborhood itself, the residents, and with other institutions (and not just judicial ones). What's constructed is *another* set of relations.

M: What I mean is that the ideal would be that we have power and thus justice will be different. But this is a long way off. Thus, to break with this "if there is no justice there is escrache" doesn't seem like a good idea.

I think that it's important not to get stuck on the idea that justice is bourgeois and thereby blind ourselves to the tools that this gives us to put these guys away. What we create is a *parallel* justice that isn't superimposed on institutional justice, and there's not necessarily a contradiction between the institutional and the social. Because of this, I don't think that we should stop demanding "an end of the laws of impunity" and "justice and punishment"; however, I think that we have to create social justice in the neighborhoods, with the people, in order to recreate bonds of solidarity. And so that justice doesn't just mean that some guy hands down a sentence, but instead that people judge for themselves what happened with their history and their country.

M: I agree with the hypothesis that says that the escrache is a practice that "seizes us." This is what we mean when we say that the escrache has a life of its own. In this way, it seems to me that beyond whatever we say about the escrache, it's certain that the escrache rejects the justice of the system. And when the escrache is, when it comes to a neighborhood, there is nothing else but the justice it unfolds. We don't discuss all of this. We work with popular justice, which does not refer to anything but itself. Perhaps in our discourses we ask for "justice and punishment," but in the escrache the justice we practice is popular, social, from below. That is, beyond what we ourselves think, the escrache is what it is: popular justice. This is what's real, because the escrache itself is more forceful than any speech or any plan.

M: The question, then, is not whether to change the slogan "justice and punishment," but rather how to think about the changes in practice occurring with the escrache.

M: But I don't consider the escrache to be only a practice, if we understand by practice the act of intervening in a neighborhood. I believe Situaciones proposed this in one of the hypotheses: that the escrache is practice but also thought. So for that reason I wouldn't separate ideal justice from real or existing justice. Because the escrache, thought of as a process, is not just the march, but rather a genuine social protagonism, which is distinct from a politics that delegates to the institution the job of producing justice. Thus, what is fundamental is the possibility that the escrache creates for thinking, today, about the construction of the social with the people. Whether or not Videla is put in jail, I'm going to be happy.[2] However, this does not mean that the escrache and its work of social condemnation should be institutionalized, but rather that its true motive is protagonism and the construction of the social.

M: I believe that we have to be careful to not become like institutional justice. That is, we should not go to the people

---

[2] *Trans.* Jorge Rafael Videla was appointed commander-in-chief of the Argentinean Army in 1975 by Isabel Perón and was one of the key members of the coup d'état that then overthrew Perón in 1976. He is also remembered for his 1975 statement: "As many people as necessary must die in Argentina so that the country can again be secure."

and say: "justice is the escrache." Because if we do that thirty of us are creating justice *for the neighbors* and that is something that they must do for themselves.

M: Yes, because the alternative is to think that social condemnation is something that we construct and that we bring to each neighborhood. But social condemnation is constructed with the neighbors and it doesn't begin or end with the escrache. Rather it materializes within it and it assumes both previous work and work to come.

M: I believe that the escrache is changing because it has changed how many people think of politics. Which is what one of the hypotheses says, because if the escrache was only a reaction to the system, I believe that we would immediately exhaust ourselves. And precisely moving away from these terms—if it's efficient, inefficient, or inept—is what enables us to make politics today. I think that if we weren't able to conceive of another way of understanding politics then we'd be in a party and we'd not be in the neighborhoods, experiencing the singularity and nuances of each community. In reality, I'm not really sure where the change began.

M: The escrache, as one of the hypotheses says, self-produces and self-affirms its own thinking on an on-going basis. Its starting point is the immobility which a belief in representative justice confines us to. And from here another form of justice is born, one that we're not really sure what it is. That's why I took notice when someone said before that we "come to re-affirm the condemnation . . . ."; no, it's not that, because what is created is something new and the forms of judging vary between the neighborhoods. There are many ways to escrache and ours is just one of them. Thus, what we generate with the escrache is a "from here on forward," a starting point. For this reason, it doesn't make any sense to talk about an opposition between this justice and that justice.

M: Furthermore, the fact that we left the downtown and went into the neighborhoods doesn't mean that we don't run up against power. Because power exists in the neighborhoods and we'd be lying if we said that everyone applauds after an escrache. Some do, yes, but others would like to beat the shit out of us. What we find is another form of power, which is not the well-known, centralized power, but rather something more complicated.

M: For me, one of the coolest changes that has taken place in the escrache is that it no longer acts in "opposition to." As a result, we are the ones who decide when to create an escrache. Thus, they don't take place only when there is an anniversary or when Crónica TV reports some piece of news about Massera or Colores or when Judge Bonadío sticks Galtieri in prison. We decide on our own time. Our time no longer belongs to the media, it no longer belongs to the emergency, rather we take the time we need to properly prepare the escrache in the neighborhood, even if it takes two or three months.

Also important is that we've changed the type of places we're working in: we no longer go to Tribunales, to the Plaza de Mayo, or to the Congress, places where we don't even know if anyone will be present. We don't go and say, "Hey man, listen to this." Instead, we use our own methods to make what we think is justice. This means that we've stopped waiting and that we are now the protagonists who choose where, how, when, and with whom we'll make justice. Because it doesn't make sense to always position ourselves with respect to the enemy: when the enemy says "white," we, to fight against it, say "black." This allows the enemy to define the terrain. It's an incredible amount of work to do this, to be the ones who determine the terrain.

2. THE GENERALIZATION

M: I think it's important to discuss how we combat the tendency towards the neutralization of the escrache. For us, it's a question of what we don't want the escrache to be. One day we discussed this in the Mesa and some really good points were raised about how we view the escraches of the assemblies or those the unions used to do or the one they did at the Torre de los Ingleses,[3] or when someone is attacked and they call this escrache. I think it's important to discuss this because it directly concerns how we understand the specificity of our practice and how we resist, as one hypothesis says, facile imitation and virtualization. I think that frequently these other escraches are not at all radical or subversive because they turn the escrache into a method.

M: But that was how HIJOS escrache began. Why shouldn't we give the same leeway to the assemblies?

M: But that's not how HIJOS escraches began. They were definitely not a *copy*. HIJOS' escraches re-invented everything from the bottom up. But then came the parties, the unions, the people who were accustomed to thinking in terms of *models* and they distorted it. And if the escrache

---

[3] *Trans.* The Torre de los Ingleses is a monument located in Retiro, which serves as a major urban and inter-urban transportation hub for Buenos Aires. This zone also houses the offices of the majority of large, international corporations. In this escrache, the monument was incorporated as a symbol for the Argentinean rejection of British oppression and influence (a key part of nineteenth century Argentinean history).

modifies itself it's because it sees that there are other areas to develop. But I don't think that the first escrache of Patria Libre[4] in the Torre de los Ingleses is the same thing as the first escrache of HIJOS against Magnacco.[5] And it's not a matter of giving these groups more time to see if they can actually do something interesting with the form of the escrache.

M: But when an assembly does an escrache against a supermarket, I don't think it's the same thing.

M: I don't know, what do you guys think? I think that we have to force ourselves to talk with the assemblies about what the escrache is for us. Because we shouldn't keep quiet about what the escrache *means* for us either because we sympathize with them or to avoid confrontation. On the contrary, we need to work on it with them.

M: But it's one thing to debate it and another to say to them that we think what they do is worthless. Because there are many ways of taking up the escrache and no one should become the arbitrator of how it should be done.

---

[4] *Trans.* Patria Libre is a left political party, in the Guevarist vein, who are active, although not central, participants in the current Kirchner government. The difference then is other groups just treat the escrache like a traditional protest, while the escraches of HIJOS work to involve the neighborhood, transform public space, and found a new type of justice.

[5] *Trans.* Jorge Luis Magnacco, a doctor at the Navy School of Mechanics, was charged and convicted of having stolen babies from political prisoners during the dictatorship.

M: That's fine, but that's just a more polite way of saying the same thing. The point is that, for me, simply to stand in front of Edesur is not an escrache.[6]

M: It's true that the escrache is not a *method*. The hypothesis that says that the escrache doesn't mimic, but rather makes a commitment is right on. What one says, one does. But when it's seen as a technique, as something that serves to, for example, attract the media, these people don't realize that in those three minutes they appear on TV, there won't be any record at all of the *real work* the escrache requires. They don't realize that to *escrache* is not the same as to *denounce*. And I don't mean to say that there is anything bad about denouncing, because denouncing is a concrete confrontation with impunity. Rather that the escrache is much more than this, meaning it's the relationships with the assemblies, the schools, the cultural centers, and the neighbors. In the analysis that we do of each escrache, for example, we don't discuss how much attention we got from the media. An escrache can be completely successful without appearing on television.

In fact, we saw problems in an earlier escrache for which we had distributed 25,000 flyers, made thousands of posters, and put thousands of letters beneath doors and in mailboxes. The entire neighborhood was informed that there was a genocidist there. But afterwards we realized

---

[6] *Trans.* Edesur is a private power and light company. After the privatization of the state-run electric company, Edesur became the primary supplier of electricity to Buenos Aires. In 2001 and 2002, there were a wave of "escraches" against Edesur and various supermarkets by neighborhood assemblies in order to protest poor service or price hikes. The speaker is criticizing the assemblies for missing the point that the escraches are not about "protest" but rather transformation and the creation of new forms of justice.

that we understood little about the neighborhood and had worked very little with their experiences. Thus the question is: what do we mean when we talk about *going into* a neighborhood?

M: I think here we return to the idea that we can't think of ourselves as a practice that defines itself in opposition to the system, like a *mirror*. Because if what the dictatorship did was to impose certain values—those of social discipline—and if it succeeded in breaking social bonds because, among other things people were complicit, then what the escrache does is to repair those bonds and to generate new values. I think it's good that the word escrache is circulating today, but the principle risk is that the escrache then becomes part of traditional politics. Because the escrache is not another form of politics; it is social protagonism at its best. That is, there is no delegating. The escrache follows a logic that is not that of a "new politics" nor of a revolutionary politics that wants to seize power and that is directed at the centers of power. In the escrache, there is an affirmation, a positivity, which is key and which does not get represented in the media.

I want to say that it's the formula, the copy, the imitation that almost always rings false because they are nothing more than "politics." Because they only value the practice in relation to power and not in relation to its opposite, which is social protagonism.

M: I think we're talking about three different things. On one hand, it's important to realize that the media uses the word escrache to describe any old act; thus, when they speak of escrache, they speak of *nothing*. But it is another thing when many people unite to *escrache* against what they consider insupportable, for example, when there is an escrache against Menem or Cavallo or against a corporation.[7] I think this is great, even if those escraches don't imply all that we do, all the work beforehand that is linked with other spaces, etc. The third thing is discussing our practice, what it means, what it specifies. These are, especially the latter two, very different things. For this reason, we shouldn't burden them with value judgments or reproaches. And it's not just a question of semantics; it concerns our own practice, like how to position ourselves in relation to the assemblies or the parties. Thus, it's not about whether or not the true escrache is enacted by HIJOS, because amongst ourselves we have created a process . . . the emergence of the Mesa de Escrache Popular shows that the escrache has been opened and that we can't simply say that it just belongs to HIJOS. This means that this is not a problem of *naming*. Because in the Mesa there is a wonderful heterogeneity of collectives and people and it's the work we do that gives us a certain identity, an identity created by putting into practice the escrache.

M: Well, I'd say that the way that the escrache doesn't close off concepts is something new. And so it seems strange to say that "this is not an escrache, because the escrache is done in this manner." What the Mesa does, which is very interesting, is to open up the idea of the escrache to include

---

[7] *Trans.* In 1991, Domingo Cavallo was appointed Minister of Economy (a post he held until July 1996). Cavallo implemented the disastrous convertibility plan that pegged the Argentine peso to the US dollar and lead the privatization of Argentina's public enterprises during the same period. He was again appointed Minister of Economy in March 2001 and was forced to resign, along with then-President De la Rúa and the rest of his cabinet, after the popular insurrection on December 19th and 20th of that same year.

different forms of interpretation. But this discussion is really about the meaning of *self-affirmation*, and because of this, I don't think you can limit what the escrache is. You have to talk with the assemblies and not only to tell them what the escrache is, but also to open it up for re-interpretation. And thus, when there is a media-centric escrache of some celebrity-hungry politician, we can't say that this is not an escrache, but rather that it's another escrache.

That is, what we need to break with is this idea that the escrache is a universal concept. And it's difficult, because you need a really strong practice of self-affirmation to sustain this heterogeneity. But the difficult and rewarding part is working with each other and, above all, with the neighbors, because it creates a strange fusion, which opens the practice, rather than shaping it or giving it a form.

M: For me, it's not important to question the use of the term but rather to ask what's the point of the escrache. I think the neighborhood assembly, in occupying this house that we currently work out of, is doing something much closer to an escrache than any of the neighborhood escraches against Edesur. It's more radical because they are doing it on their own terms: they occupy the space and begin to work and to create something that didn't exist before out of this occupied house where we're working right now and where other movements now work from as well. Something much more interesting than any escrache is going on here. Thus, it's not important to debate which is the real escrache, but rather to understand *what* creates change and what maintains the status quo. There are many escraches that don't change anything, that are conservative, and therefore it doesn't interest me if they are done by the assemblies or by an idol of mine.

In fact a collective, like the Paternal assembly,[8] could do everything right and tomorrow create a horrible escrache. And we also could do something quite old and unoriginal that has no effect at all. Thus, I think that the conversation is not about *who* does it, but rather *what* is done.

To return to one of the hypotheses: it's the escrache that "seizes us" without a concern for who makes us. It's a process, a practice that transforms and inspires us to work towards the same goal. Therefore, the act is more important than the actors. In this sense, it's important to think about this process; because it's not simply about, for example, creating an escrache at a factory or at a warehouse. Here I'm talking about escraches that we ourselves, as HIJOS and the Mesa, have done. It's not merely a question of who is involved.

One possibility is to think: "The escrache is resignified when it's taken up by someone else." But, in reality, that just gives others carte blanche to do any old shit. For me, it doesn't necessarily resignify. Rather, in general, it just mimics an empty method, while at other times it generates an action that is deeply conservative in nature. For example, three militants get together, wave the flag, call Crónica TV, and create an escrache. And that is considered a resignification? No; for me that *devalues* something that is interesting.

For this reason, I think the assemblies are related to the escrache. For example, they take one of COTO's parking lots and convert it into a public space, into a plaza.[9] That is

---

[8] *Trans.* Paternal is a neighborhood in Buenos Aires, and the assembly of Paternal is one of the many assemblies that emerged during 2002 and that so altered the social and political landscape of Argentina. The assembly took over a house where the Mesa de Escrache met while organizing an escrache in Paternal.

[9] *Trans.* COTO is an Argentinean supermarket chain. In this escrache, the neighbors in the assembly of Villa Urquiza, occupied

what interests me about the assemblies and not this debate about whether we should give them time to see if they can put together a good escrache.

M: Ours is a concrete practice that attempts to connect up with something that has been damaged or destroyed, like ties between neighbors in a certain area. The values that our work deals with are justice, impunity, and condemnation. This is a point that connects our first conversation with Situaciones—where we differentiated between the just and justice—to this one and the escrache's generalization. And our experience has changed how we now think about justice and has created a space for different interpretations. But we want to highlight its potential, and not, as has happened in other cases, its limitations. To escrache Menem, for example, has a point, but it's also a hollow action, because it does not incorporate the baggage of all those decades, which is exactly what gets put into play when we work in a neighborhood.

3. ASSEMBLIES

M: I'd like to ask a question. In the third hypothesis, what does "hypothesis-in-practice" mean?

Situaciones: A hypothesis-in-practice is the opposite of a universal method applied to a set of local conditions. A method is applied to a *case*, and *cases* are what we call singular things after they have lost their singularity. Cases, unlike the objects or events they stand in for, are completely interchangeable. When such a method is applied, then, the

---

the parking lot of a local COTO in order to prevent the supermarket from illegally taking over an adjacent piece of land to expand the lot.

universality that is put into play is an abstract universality. Here, there is no such thing as a situation, an irreducible singularity, nor is working from within it a possibility. A hypothesis-in-practice begins, on the contrary, from the recognition of a singular situation, of a concrete universality[10] in which it's unknown *a priori* what the consequences of an intervention will be. But this "state of unknowing" is not ignorance, but rather a call for an investigation from within the situation: an investigation-in-practice, employing one or several hypotheses-in-practice. In this sense, a hypothesis is simply the carrying out of a practice to see what it will then produce.

For example, it was not immediately apparent that the children of the disappeared would develop a new process of justice; namely, the escrache of the genocidists. Nor was it clear what would happen when they did this and even less whether this practice was going to necessitate corrections or displacements once it had been placed into action. That's why we say the escrache is a hypothesis-in-practice, because in a given situation it produces a vector, a trajectory, placing something in motion in the real world that one must then watch and correct depending on what it produces. Until it happens, one can't know its effects or its trajectory.

---

[10] *Trans.* This is a passing reference to Hegel as read by Zizek. "This, then, is the Hegelian 'concrete universality': at every stage of the dialectical process, the concrete figure 'colours' the totality of the process, i.e. the universal frame of the process becomes part of (or, rather, drawn into) the particular content. To put it in Ernesto Laclau's terms, at every stage its particular content is not only a subspecies of the universality of the total process: it 'hegemonises' this very universality, the 'dialectical process' is nothing but the name for this permanent shift of the particular content which 'hegemonises' the universality" (Slavoj Zizek, *The Fright of Real Tears*, London: British Film Institute, pp. 23-24).

There is not a universal method that makes it possible. A universal method produces a general, strategic knowledge, one that always knows what's lacking in a situation (and the "correct" line to walk), but, in the end, it always comes up short. Instead, what we see today are groups working within a given situation that observe what works and what doesn't. And it's always, in the beginning, an independent investigation because *the one who thinks it, does it*, instead of (as the strategists would have it) the subordination of those who do to those who think.

In this way, we begin to discover the possibilities of a hypothesis-in-practice and what it does well, since it alone never guarantees success. Rather the idea of success is always defined by the group, and not by an outside observer who hands down a verdict from some privileged place.

Therefore, following this line of thought, we believe that the notion of *transversality* is important for the escrache to the extent that the escrache rearticulates subject positions in a situation. It doesn't direct itself "at" the workers, "at" doormen, "at" students, as pre-established, fixed identities, as those who it has to bring together as they are. Instead, the escrache activates a nucleus of meanings—specific to each neighborhood—which are linked to an as-yet unresolved injustice. This commonly held injustice is what makes it so that a worker doesn't have to go as a worker, nor a Trotskyite as a Trotskyite, but rather that, in the escrache, each person is involved via the transversality found in this injustice.

M: In this sense, I don't think we can say very much about the issue of our relationship to the assemblies because we're right now in the midst of constructing this relationship. We're currently discovering ways of working with them and this process is on-going.

S: But then, for you all, what does an escrache of the Mesa have in common with what the assemblies do?

M: When we made our second attempt to create an escrache in Villa Urquiza there was already an assembly there which was very mobilized.[11] The escrache's role is to reconstruct broken social bonds but it turned out that we were going into a neighborhood where there were already groups of neighbors working together. It looked as if our objective was already in place. Thus many things had to change: how do we now deal with the neighborhood? From what angle? And what is our relation to this group which has already created a network in the neighborhood?

What resulted was a big change, an almost idyllic change. This change occurred between when we were planning the escrache for December 19th (which was then suspended) and when we picked the escrache up again in February. The contrast was notable.

I think that at first we didn't know how to deal with it. And it was a process of discovery that was, for us, overwhelming because suddenly what we had hoped to achieve was already in place and the question now was "what next?"

---

[11] This refers to the escrache of Cardinal Juan Carlos Aramburu which should have originally taken place on the evening of December 19, 2001. At the moment, a state of siege in Argentina was imminent as a response to the generalized looting of supermarkets. Those who were going to participate gathered at a corner in the neighborhood of Villa Urquiza where the escrache was supposed to take place, but a decision was taken to suspend it. Hours before many of these people had participated in the protests that set off the December insurrection (see *19 y 20, Apuntes para el nuevo protagonismo social,* De mano en mano, April 2002). The escrache finally took place on March 23rd of 2002, and it was directed as well at Roberto Alemann, the ex-Minister of Economy during Galtieri's dictatorship and a cheerleader for neoliberal reforms.

The paradox is that in our last escrache, which took place in Paternal, the relationship to the assembly was very strange because a deep bond was never formed.[12] Thus, it was a new experience. It was as if we were sizing each other up. Because without a doubt we wanted to work together, but we had to see how it would come about.

M: I think that, in terms of practice, we have a lot in common, primarily concerning the appearance of new forms of politics that reject representation. Between the escrache and its rejection of institutional justice and the "they all must go" there are many similarities.[13] There is also the problem of horizontality: the Mesa and the assemblies both work with a really heterogeneous set of ideas.

Before, when we came to a neighborhood, the first thing we did was to find the plaza and start working alongside the cultural centers and neighborhood groups. This time we came to a plaza that was already occupied by an assembly in a neighborhood in which they were already working. This forced us to reconsider how the escrache was going to work, why we were going to the neighborhoods. It caused a crisis.

For example, it's really fascinating that in San Cristóbal, before the 19th and the 20th, we worked quite well with the neighborhood groups which had existed prior to the

---

[12] On August 3, 2002 there was an escrache of Ricardo Scifo Módica (aka) "Alacran," whose address is 1955 Condarco in the neighborhood of La Paternal. Alacran is free thanks to the immunity granted under the *Punto Final* law passed by the government of Raúl Alfonsin. He worked in the "Club Atlético," "El Olmpo," and "El Banco" detention centers. Between the years 1991 to 1996, he worked as the director of the Center for Victims of Sexual Harrasment of the Argentine Federal Police.

[13] *Trans.* This is the slogan that spontaneously arose and circulated during and after the events of December 19 and 20, 2001.

assemblies.[14] But here in Paternal it was very difficult to join forces with them. There wasn't a relationship.

I believe that in part the reason was that a dynamic already existed in the neighborhood. And then we show up with a parallel dynamic, which was not the principle one, and it was hard for us to stop ourselves and watch what was developing.

M: I would place it in a more pessimistic light because we didn't know how to work with the assemblies. We don't know. In retrospect, we can say it was a total failure.

We went to the office of the assembly and we went to the plaza where there was another assembly, but we had practically no dialogue with any of them. It seemed to me like we were going around with blinders on and we couldn't stop to see what was happening. Like we were exterminators that came, worked, and then left. And we thought we just needed to become hegemonic, to add people to our project. Because until then we always came with the new, the novel, and we worked with the neighborhood on something that we knew how to do.

All of a sudden these people appeared who were doing interesting things and we didn't know how to relate to them. We thought: now that there are assemblies, what a year we're going to have! And for nothing. It was really difficult. To begin with, it's very difficult to stop thinking only about yourself, to think that there are other people doing things, people with whom we didn't get along and with whom we

---

[14] There was an escrache of Miguel Angel Rovira in the neighborhood of San Cristóbal on September 8, 2001. Rovira's address is 1032 Pasco. He is accused of 27 murders and of being one of the principal members of Triple A. At the time of the escrache, he was working as Chief of Security for the subway firm Metrovias. For more information see HIJOS, #12, Summer 2002.

couldn't work. I think we arrived with the model of what we wanted to do and we didn't want to abandon that and have to think that perhaps there are other things which could be more interesting. Many people in HIJOS felt threatened.

4. IDENTITY

M: In the beginning the escraches were driven by HIJOS But once they began to take shape the Mesa de Escrache was created, which was a collective of new and previously unaffiliated people. And this collective gradually took over the task of organization, which was done horizontally, where no one person holds more decision-making power than any other.[15]

S: And what was this transformation like, as it seems to have been a transformation in identity for the group? The transformation from "*hijos*" as victims to HIJOS who propose a hypotheses-in-practice like the escrache. A transformation that perhaps includes the way in which HIJOS's original idea has "emptied out" so that "any person" can feel like they are a *hijo* by participating in the escrache and, in this way, can participate in a shared history.

M: I think this has to do with the fact that the escrache is something which defines itself in positive terms. And, for this reason, it has been able to transcend its original identity, which has mutated and transformed, and to recreate itself with other groups and people. It's that the escrache is

---

[15] *Trans.* This refers to the organizational structure of the assemblies, which are organized horizontally as opposed to hierarchically. In practical terms, it means that in a given organization there are no fixed jobs, and no "leaders" institutionalized as such, rather participants cycle through all the positions within the organization—the idea being both to distribute power and to disrupt the division of labor inherent to capitalism.

not merely a negation of the damage suffered, but rather an activity with positive purposes, such as social condemnation and popular justice.

M: A clear example of how the escrache has transcended HIJOS can be seen in the creation of the Mesa de Escrache. For members of HIJOS, after the creation of the Mesa, we were able to displace ourselves from the center of the organization and thus see ourselves as just one more member of the Mesa. This put us all on the same level, both for the discussions and the actual work. The importance of this decision was that we realized that the escrache does not have a creator, that no one owns it, and that it's something we build together.

M: This arrangement is critical, because without it there would be no possibility to work with social condemnation, since this work needs the active involvement of the people and of the residents. Without this structure, we would have remained stuck on a very specific demand.

M: Many people were into this idea of enacting justice, of social condemnation, that goes hand-in-hand with working in the neighborhoods and this goes beyond what was originally started by HIJOS. But it's more than this, it's that this move to working for social condemnation transgresses all kinds of limits and structures, including the Mesa de Escrache itself.

M: I believe that identity is not something fixed or inherited, rather it's always in motion. And that in the displacement of the role of HIJOS—first as creator and founder of the escrache and now as part of the Mesa—our identity went through several changes. I think this is seen in the altering of our original slogan, "justice and punishment," to the one we use more now, "social condemnation." This shift has to do with the fact that identity becomes established through the struggle. For this reason, I think everyone can be a "hijo."

Moreover, I think it's interesting what was said earlier about when an assembly occupies a space that this is closer to being like an escrache than when an assembly actually creates an "escrache."

M: I would like to bring up what we discussed on March 24th, when marching with the banner of the Mesa came up. One idea that we touched on that day was that our identity is basically defined by being in the neighborhood and working on an escrache; that is, we are only the Mesa de Escrache when we are planning an escrache in a given neighborhood. I think it's great that the Mesa can be something extremely heterogeneous, which can be seen in many of our discussions and that this identity is based in the practice of the escrache.

M: Another one of the conversations that affected us took place last year just as the Mesa was starting to take on more of a leading role, when we began to prepare speeches and other small things that before were handled only by HIJOS. We were preparing the escrache of Rovira, and the participation of the Mesa was increasing with each escrache, but HIJOS was still in charge of coordinating the overall event. It was said then that the escrache belonged more to HIJOS than to the other participants, that it belonged more to HIJOS than to society as a whole. And HIJOS continued to provide the cash needed to fund the escrache. In a debate, the question was raised that if the escrache indeed belonged to everyone, then it must belong to everyone at all levels. For it seemed as if autonomy was being detached from the problem of economically sustaining the escrache:

autonomy was more a right that belonged to those of us who participated in the Mesa than a responsibility that needed to be sustained. The question was how to create a space in which we all felt equal when one organization was supplying 90% of the cash.

I think that this was a conversation that marked a turning point, because we then began to do many things as the Mesa: parties, raffles. . . . And from this point on I think all of our mindsets changed, which goes to show that economics really is important.

M: I entered in November of last year, with the escrache of Yedro, and my experience as a militant grew with my involvement in the Mesa.[16] At first it was all very functional: where to pass out flyers, how to hang posters, etc. But starting in March a change took place, which corresponded with a big crisis in the Mesa and a serious discussion about what we wanted, how to manage ourselves, and about the necessity of beginning to *produce*. At that point, an archive was created, as well as a committee to launch a magazine, whose first issue has already been published.[17] We threw a party in February that brought in a lot of money which has kept us afloat until now. I think that from that moment on the Mesa I matured quite a bit, and the escrache as

---

[16] This refers to the escrache of Juan Martín Yedro who lives at 698 PB 6, Apt. B, Palestina Avenue in the neighborhood of Paternal. Yedro is a subofficial in the Armada Conadep 1080, which to this day boasts of having participated in tortures and murders in the School of Mecánica de la Armada (ESMA) and in the *vuelos de la muerte* ("flights of death"). He presently works for the Secretariat of State Intelligence and is head of the cultural center "Los Amigos" at 658 Palestina, 1st floor. His telephone number is 4865-8879.

[17] *Piedra Libre,* the magazine of the Mesa de Escrache Popular, first published in July 2002.

well, because I think that our identity is a joint creation of the Mesa, HIJOS, and the neighborhood. When HIJOS became a part of the Mesa (which happened in November of last year), it stopped being the only group to organize and operate the escrache. And I think it's far more productive working like this because we are learning more.

M: I believe that beyond the identity of each group that participates in the Mesa—and this was something we discussed with a colleague who came from the FUNA in Chile and who went with us to a neighborhood—what gives identity to the escrache is the everyday work that we do in the neighborhoods, because here is where all the identities that the escrache takes up and transforms are located.[18]

M: For this reason the act of entering a new neighborhood transforms the escrache. The escrache in Villa Urquiza didn't have much in common with the one in Paternal.[19] Ourselves, the situation, the people, the historical moment, these all continually change. Obviously, between now and last November the country has totally changed.

M: As we have stated, after the 19th and the 20th, entering the neighborhoods is no longer the same. Above all because of the assemblies. And, at the same time, we have also changed quite a bit as a result of the conversations that took

---

[18] *Trans.* An organization from Chile, similar to HIJOS, that creates escrache-like actions known as *funa* to protest the disappearances that occurred under Pinochet. The term *funa* is the (imaginary) noun derived from the Chilean slang term funar which can mean to observe, fuck, or threaten with a beating or death. The adjective form *estar funado* (to be fucked, said of someone who you are threatening, roughly) is also common.

[19] *Trans.* A well-known neighborhood in Buenos Aires.

place last March. These conversations were the result of two escraches from December of last year: one that was coming along well in a neighborhood and the other which was to be part of an homage to the priests of the Third World. However, with the second there wasn't time to prepare it correctly.

S: For the "hijos" who participate in the escraches, when there are conversations with HIJOS, what's their experience like?

M: It's contradictory. Beyond being conscious of what is implied in the construction of social condemnation—which has been and will continue to be the focus of our work—it's not easy to accept and become responsible for the fact that the escrache transcends us as a group. Above all, because the escrache as a practice has evolved quite a bit and now I think we need to begin rethinking our slogans of "social condemnation" and "escrache popular." Particularly, as a member of HIJOS, I'm presented with the dichotomy of either continuing to demand "justice and punishment" or focusing more on the concept of "popular justice" and all that is involved in the work being done in the neighborhoods: the daily labor, the interactions with the neighbors, the bonds of solidarity.

Even though HIJOS is part of the Mesa now, the Mesa has a very particular and well-defined role that is shared with a series of collectives and people. These groups come together in the escrache. HIJOS, by contrast, as an association has a series of activities that are all of a piece, part of one strategy, of a unified message. However, the escrache can no longer be determined by needs outside of the neighborhoods. If not, we risk devaluing it or aborting the construction of the social condemnation. This work is work from the bottom up.

The way that the escrache has taken off has generated some tension. On the one hand, we want the escrache to transcend, to be for everyone. On the other hand, it sometimes appears that it's "slipping out of our hands" and that "it can't be contained." I think that we all want social condemnation, but it's difficult to admit that the escrache is already something that transcends both HIJOS and the Mesa. It's better to think of the escrache as incarnated each time by more and more people and if these people feel like the escrache is theirs, then it's a victory for HIJOS.

M: Beginning with the discussions that we had in March, the Mesa matured a great deal. We were forced to talk about many things that we didn't before, and in that sense it was very good. We began to talk about how each of us understood the escrache.

And it wasn't an easy conversation, because the problem of defining the dates for escraches or dealing with financing are things that should come from the Mesa, from where the escrache is being developed.

M: This crisis revived the Mesa when we had to take responsibility for the fact that the escrache could no longer respond to conditions that weren't part of the neighborhood. These two escraches (from December of last year) one after the other went against what had been the logic of the escraches, went against its sense of timing, its form, the preparation and the way that the escrache had established itself in the neighborhoods . . . like it was a part of them, building from the inside, and not just dropping in like an unwanted guest. We felt strongly that something had gone wrong in the back-to-back escraches and this forced us to reexamine many things.

S: Why was the December 19th escrache suspended?

M: It was a combination of things. A state of siege was about to be declared, the people were going to the Plaza de Mayo, and we didn't know what was going on. It was a decision we made in the street, on the corner of Pampa and Triunvirato . . . the people were already there and we were preparing to escrache Aramburu.[20]

M: No, it wasn't like that. First, it was suspended by HIJOS, who had met up in the street, and then they spoke to the Mesa.

S: But why? What were they thinking?

M: We concluded that as a political act it was pointless. It didn't make sense to do an escrache at that particular moment when there was looting going on everywhere.

M: And in addition to the looting there were deaths. We decided to suspend it because of security issues and because the escrache would have been pointless in this context.

M: As well, there were only a few people that day. Because of the state of siege there were only three hundred people, and we thought that if the escrache took place on a normal day there would probably be about a thousand people. Moreover, we wouldn't have been able to do it properly, so pushing the date back gave us the possibility to explore the implications of the escraches. In the end, that was what happened.

---

[20] *Trans.* Cardinal Juan Carlos Aramburu was the Archbishop of Buenos Aires from 1975 to 1990. He is seen as a figure who, while not directly complicit with the dictatorship, turned a blind eye towards its abuses and who has refused to acknowledge them to this day.

S: When the escrache was suspended, did you separate or stay together to see what would happen?

M: At that moment everything was totally crazy. But most of us took a bus together and went to the HIJOS house.

S: And did you go together to the protest that evening?

M: No, HIJOS proposed an assembly with all the different organizations that were around: the Mesa de escrache, GAC, and SIMECA.[21] Most of us stayed at the HIJOS house; others returned to their homes or participated in the protests.

5. RESISTING VIRTUALIZATION

M: I think it's important to point out that this "failed" escrache was a media-centric one: cameras had to be present. This has been a topic of conversation for us, because there are participants in the Mesa who think that there is no contradiction between a media-based escrache and a neigh-

---

[21] *Trans.* The Grupo de Arte Callejero (GAC) was founded in 1999 and, since its inception, has played an important role in the organization and development of the escraches. One of their principle methods of production involves working from within or in tandem with social movements, producing manifestations, signs and posters, and alterations in public space during marches, etc. The GAC first came to international attention when they were included in the 2002 Documenta; they have since stopped exhibiting in museum and gallery spaces. SIMECA is Sindicato de Mensajeros y Cadetes (the Union of Messengers and Cadets), more commonly known as "motoqueros." They also participated in the Mesa de Escrache Popular.

borhood-based escrache, while others think that we should do a combination of the two.

M: The escrache that was to take place on December 19th was conceived with the media in mind. HIJOS had decided that this escrache would be part of an homage to the priests of the Third World. And it was necessary to escrache those parts of the Church that were complicit. In this sense, it had to be media-centric. But the Mesa proposed that it shouldn't be media-centric, that it should focus instead on working in a neighborhood.

For us this all took place really rapidly, we had to split up and re-evaluate because there was something that was not quite right.

M: And the escrache against Aramburu was to complement the escrache of the Third World priests. The escrache was like the cherry on top; it was decorative and media-centric.

M: I think that now all of us in the Mesa believe the escrache should be a neighborhood construction because each time it becomes more and more about social condemnation. And a media-based escrache doesn't contribute much to our understanding of social condemnation.

M: I don't agree, because I don't think this issue is settled. I think that a lot of times our actions are determined by our needs. There are moments when we're not doing anything, not working on any escraches, and if the idea of a media-centric escrache comes up we can begin to work on it and later see how we can recruit the neighborhood. This is something that we have to continue to work on.

S: But what is the difference between these two types of escraches?

M: It has to do with what is privileged. In one, the media and the amount of people who go to the event are key; in the other, it's the weekends spent in the neighborhood, the work done with the neighbors, with the guy who runs the newsstand, with the people you meet and talk to. There is, in each, a different assessment of the meaning of the escrache; in the Mesa, one of the most important ideas is that the neighbors are the prison.

Moreover, when one does a media-centric escrache one legitimizes the media as agents of justice because they disseminate the denunciation. Even though this issue is not completely settled, it has made us realize that the media doesn't legitimize our practice. And this, in turn, leads to another question: what *does* legitimize an escrache? What is the subject of an escrache?

M: I think the difference between the two is very clear. In a media-centric escrache the media plays the critical role, and the neighbors and the neighborhood are passive elements. In a neighborhood-centered escrache, it's the opposite: the media is nothing more than what their name implies, a medium, an instrument. These are two ways of talking with the people. One implies one set of conditions and the other, another.

M: A media-centric escrache is an invitation to *watch* what we do . . . it's something closer to a show, but it's not an invitation to participate in and construct the escrache. When we first started we would plan an escrache in a neighborhood for 9:00 and then we would descend on the neighborhood like aliens from another planet at 8:30. In fact, many of the neighbors would watch us on TV because the idea was to arrive at 8:30 so that we would appear on the nightly news.

M: But now we know that the day of the march is the culmination of the escrache and that the escrache is really part of working with the neighborhood. For example, the work we did in Paternal was impressive. Before the march we went by his house twice. We had a huge turnout. The neighbors notified us at one point that his cronies had covered all the posters, and these old ladies told us who did it. This guy was more than escrached on the day of the march.

M: Having said this, even though we go around saying that the escrache is a process, when we buy the newspaper the next day and we're not in it, the truth is that it's a little annoying. And if a little note appears saying that only two hundred people came and not one thousand, that also pisses us off (*laughter*). It takes awhile to become unattached. It takes a lot of work to stop being dependent on the little smile you get from reading the newspaper on Sunday.

M: I think this is what came out of our last evaluation session when we weren't satisfied because we didn't know how to work with the assemblies. And this crisis occurred because we were working more and more in the neighborhoods. If a media-centric escrache was our top priority, then it would be enough to simply send a newsletter to the assemblies. If this were the case then these problems and concerns would simply not exist.

S: In deciding not to work for the media, does this imply that you are no longer trying to work with the majority of people?

M: No, because while part of the escrache is its dissemination, the escrache is more than just that dissemination. In this sense, it's not media-centric . . . we don't work *for* the media, which is not to say that we don't work *with* the media. Changing the focus does not mean renunciation and isolation.

During the escrache of Almagro, journalists from Punto Doc were doing a special program about fugitives from justice, and they wanted to feature someone who was escrached.[22] They told us that they were interested in the process of the escrache. That was a lie. When they arrived, they asked us to start the escrache so that it could appear live on their program.

Thus, it's not that we don't want to work with the media, but rather we have decided that what we do is incompatible with their logic. They are interested in news and in that sense they provide information, and there's nothing wrong with that. But the escrache can't be reduced to the news; it is the work done in the neighborhood. Moreover, we work as well with other forms of communication, like letters to residents in which we explain why we are doing the escrache, what an escrache is, how it actually opposes violence and how we're not going to destroy everything.[23]

M: It's the difference between communicating and informing. The latter is what the media does. In Almagro, something happened that touches on this. Since Yedro lived in an apartment building, the neighbors were worried because they did not want their walls to be stained with paint. We had a good discussion about this, and it was very interesting because we were able to discuss the rationale for

---

[22] *Trans.* Punto Doc is an Argentine TV program.

[23] The previously cited *Piedra Libre* features a "Letter to the Neighbors," which was distributed in the neighborhood of Paternal to invite them to the escrache of Alacrán. The letter begins: "Neighbors: this is an invitation to act and think together. Because we believe that real justice is created by all of us, we invite you to construct an ESCRACHE."

why we toss the paint bombs, what this symbolic act signifies, and what the meaning of the escrache is.

S: It's clear that one of the keys to the escrache is the
reconstruction of social bonds, and thus the work in
the neighborhoods. And, on the other hand, it's important
that the escrache comes off successfully and that it be massive. Perhaps it might be good to return to one of the topics
from our first conversation; namely, how we understand the
relationship between social reconstruction and mass participation or consensus? What does it mean to reconstruct
social bonds and what type of work does this imply?

M: Mass participation, as we have said, is less and less our
main focus. It's important, but it's not what legitimizes an
escrache. The legitimization of the escrache results from
how well it engages the neighborhood. Before, we would
go to the neighborhoods at night to distribute flyers, hang
posters, paint murals, and now we go together during the
day, not to flood the area with images, but as a group, with
a drum, a megaphone, a puppet—we speak to the people
and walk through the whole of the neighborhood. We pass
through it, making noise, handing out information.

M: During our last discussion, we talked about how this
guy had really been escrached for almost three weeks before
the actual march, we discussed whether or not the "D-day"
was actually important. That's why we say that the escrache
is really just the final act in a larger process of work with
the neighborhood, and, at the same time, the beginning of
the future of the escrache, as done by the community. A
week before the last escrache we ran into a woman who told
us that she was about to recommend an English teacher to
Alacran's wife, but when she realized who she was she didn't
tell her anything.

M: In any case, it's not easy to wean yourself from what mass participation signifies. I remember the escrache we did in Lugano.[24] We had done a lot of work on it and thought that the escrache would be packed with people. However, very few people showed up and we were depressed and worried afterward.

M: I think that there is no contradiction in saying that mass participation is important. Not being media-centric is really a bet on our part that the people will stop being spectators and participate. The problem is that there are different ways of participating . . . there's the guy who talks to people while passing out flyers or someone who participates in the process but who can't come on the day of the escrache. But it's important that people come that day because it's a sign of all our work.

The analysis that took place after Lugano had to do with the following: we worked in the neighborhood, but not with the neighborhood. From that moment on the Mesa began to work out of the neighborhood where the escrache would take place, and not from the HIJOS house, because

---

[24] In the neighborhood of Lugano, there was an escrache of the murderer Rubén Osvaldo Bufano, whose address is 6236 PB 3 Madariaga. It was on December 18, 2000. Bufano was in the servicio de Inteligencia del Batallón 601, and he participated in the transfer of prisoners from ESMA center to Tigre. He worked for murderers and dictators like Leandro Anaya, Acdel Villas, and Juan Carlos Onganía. He was also a guard for the ex-governor of San Juan and he worked as an auditor for PJ Capital. He is accused of fraud, extortion, and kidnapping. In 1981, he was arrested along with two other ex-paramilitaries in Switzerland for the kidnapping of an Uruguayan banker. He said that he would give information about the kidnapping of Haroldo Conti and many others in exchange for not being extradited. He has also been accused of murder and state-sponsored terrorism by the Spanish judge Baltasar Garzón.

we realized that although we had been in the neighborhood, we didn't know the people who lived there and we didn't know what was going on there.

S: What is the difference between working *with* the neighborhood and not simply *in* the neighborhood?

M: It's a search, by those of us who are trying to move forward, who know the neighborhood, its codes and its history. If we can work *with* the neighborhood, then half of the escrache is already done, because the escrache is created by the neighborhood, not by us. It's not just dropping in out of the blue, but instead trying to understand who in the neighborhood is working, who is there building social bonds.

Mass participation is not something I can just give up. I don't think it's a traditional form of political action, rather it's the result of the work we do. We don't care so much about mass participation in terms of the media, but we want people to participate.

M: Yes, because it's a problematic to think of the escrache as something done by "the few, but the good." That's traditional politics. How many times have we seen groups on the left splinter, and the group that's left over says, "We're only two hundred, but we're the best"? It's fantastic if two thousand people come to an escrache, especially if they don't come because of the media or because they were sent by a political party. Moreover, this mass participation is then experienced as an action in the neighborhood and not through reports in the media.

S: Now what happens if you go into a neighborhood and there is not consensus about the escrache? Or if there are other forms of protagonism?

M: I'm not sure, but San Cristóbal was an interesting example. The neighbors, who had already been working together for quite some time, had organized the security, the use of toilets along the route, which were located in the homes of participating residents, and there was even an apartment from which you could see Rovira's garden—we could even see what his dog was doing. Everything was tremendously horizontal and shared. For me, it's important to acknowledge and to learn from the protagonism of the people.

M: However, it's also important to point out that the choice of who to escrache, and in what neighborhood, isn't done naively because we know that to hold an escrache in Belgrano, Palermo, or Barrio Norte is more complicated. For example, throwing 25 flyers out of a window has nothing to do with passing out flyers house-to-house. Moreover, when we are deciding which guy to escrache, we want to find someone who is already not too well-known in the media. Thus, we look for someone who is less important, who represents, perhaps even more, the idea of impunity. In other words, de-emphasizing the importance of the media is not only about an uncomfortableness with the camera, but rather it has to do with how every aspect of the escrache functions: the day, the form, the person to be escrached, the neighborhood, etc.

M: The other issue is consensus, which we can't think of as absolute agreement with what we do. There have always been people opposed to us; there have always been threats and warnings that fascist types were going to show. But the fact that there are people opposed to us has never been something that has impeded the escrache. In any case, we are more interested in what happens with those people who are neutral, who do not choose a side, who do not clearly draw a line between being a critic and an accomplice of the repressor.

M: Moreover, one gets used to searching for a consensus amongst people. However, I would have never imagined that the "justification" for an escrache would come from Alacrán himself, who, just two days ago, put his house up for sale. That's huge.

S: From one point-of-view we can clearly say that mass participation and consensus are welcome. But perhaps there is a way in which these two parameters obscure much more than they reveal. This is what we'd like to discuss.

The escrache is not only about denunciation. It also works with social condemnation and examines how to reconstruct social bonds. But the escrache itself is not social condemnation, precisely because the social condemnation involves a larger dynamic with the neighbors, etc. You yourselves warn of the danger of having a fixed model of justice that you then take to the neighborhoods.

Thus, it appears to me that when the escrache goes to a neighborhood, it is, in a certain sense, an investigation: of what social condemnation is, of how it's constructed, of how social bonds are being produced, and how these bonds are developed in each neighborhood. I think this has to do with searching for something that moves beyond mass participation and consensus because if we don't know what it means to reconstruct social bonds, then what gives value to mass participation or consensus? In other words, what do we have to examine?

Thus, keeping mass participation as a criteria for the success of an escrache is problematic, because it implies that priority is being given to the ability to communicate, to denounce, or to propose, and this can became a way of controlling what is produced.

M: I want to add something that has really affected my thinking. After the night of December 19th, what does mass participation mean anymore? Before that night, to walk through the city and see people out on the streets in that way was unthinkable. I think that after December 19th we have to think about mass participation differently. This is what happened to the assemblies: what does it mean to fill the Plaza de Mayo after the 19th?

In our case, something similar happened: we're not looking to fill the Plaza de Mayo in an escrache; instead we hope that the neighborhoods themselves will administer the condemnation. Therefore, the problem is when we see the same faces as always, when those who come to the escraches are the militant hipsters who go to all the marches, as it was at the beginning. When you see new faces, when people from the neighborhood come, this means something is happening.

S: For this reason, it's evident to me at least that the escrache cannot be measured in terms of mass participation, because it's not a problem of scale. You don't say that one number is a failure and that another number is not.

M: I agree. However, I still think that if you go to an escrache and see two hundred people it's worrisome, and when you see two thousand people it's not.

S: But why then is two thousand a good number?

M: It's not that two thousand is good because we're not so interested in mass participation quantitatively. If we were, we'd work to guarantee the number, which would mean, for example, special treatment for the political parties: they would march in the front, or something like that. But the number is an index, a figure which we evaluate even though it's not how we measure success. It's not linear; it's not that a large turnout automatically equals success. And this is why we said that even though many people came to this escrache, we weren't satisfied with what it attained.

S: This discussion has its roots in our discussion of consensus, and of course it's better to have two thousand people than two hundred, but here's the question: two thousand or two hundred what? Because a consensus tends to homogenize individuals, and this does not speak to what is produced, which is something un-quantifiable.

M: But we never go and say that an escrache was good because eight hundred people showed up. In other words, we are interested in the escrache's construction and not in its dramatic effect. Those eight hundred or two thousand people do not show up all of a sudden. Instead, they are the product of work done with the neighborhood, which sometimes turns out better and sometimes worse. The people who come have more to do with the process of construction that is the escrache and not just the call put out. You see this when you run into those people that you debated with for fifteen minutes in the street the other day. This process which we develop with the neighbors, as you can see, is not the same as the spontaneity of December 19th. It's something else altogether.

M: I think here we can see an example of the escrache's transversality. Because if we say that the escrache comes from neither the neighborhood nor the outside, but that it goes through it, then the question becomes what is it that was constructed? Here it's a question of two hundred or two thousand *what*. What do we leave behind, what do we construct, what do we carry with us?

For me, this issue of mass participation would be a problem only if we thought differently; if we dedicated ourselves to getting attention from the media; if we created a Mesa with the political parties; if our work was completely superficial and not underground. But if after all the work we do, if we evaluate mass participation as just another factor, then I don't think it's a problem. If the only important thing for us was mass participation, then we'd have to resort to using the traditional methods of politics to attract people.

But I think it's a powerful sign that we no longer see leftist posters—with Massera's face behind bars—getting the attention of the cameras at the escrache: this shows that the escrache is no longer a business, it's not a shop window for advertising your group or for boosting membership.

M: It's worth noting that we are interested less in escraches like the one against Etchecolaz,[25] where two thousand people showed up, or the one where Santillán spoke,[26] which was massive, than the ones we do in the neighborhoods and to which, in general, less people come.

---

[25] Miguel Etchecolatz lives at 1035 Pueyrredón, 9th floor. During the dictatorship, he was the Director General of Investigations of the Buenos Aires police and the right hand man of General Ramón Camps. He is the one living person most responsible for the Noche de los Lápices (name given to a series of kidnappings of university students that occurred on September 16 and 17, 1976), and he was a beneficiary of the Obedencia Debida law enacted by the government of Raúl Alfonsin. In this escrache, there was severe police repression, with tear gas, people running in fear, and many people beaten and arrested.

[26] José Alfredo Martinez de Hoz, architect of the dictatorship's economic policy, was escrached on May 1, 1998 with a mass mobilization that culminated with speeches by various union leaders, including Carlos Perro Santillán.

M: These massive turnouts happened because we were working in these left circles. But now that these "militants" have left this "market," which gave them only "low returns," points to a need to understand the *what* of mass participation, since it's not that we told them not to come, but rather they opted out.

6. VIOLENCE

S: You've read the newspapers and heard people say that the escrache is fascist. And these are not just people on the right. How do you all respond to this?

M: I think what the hypothesis says about the two political subjectivities is good. First, that of revolutionaries of the seventies who were devoted to taking power from the state and to carrying out justice from this position. And second that of democratic politics, which is where the criticism of the escrache as fascist is coming from and which shares the revolutionary subjectivity's ideas concerning the *place* of justice. Seen from this perspective, I don't think the escrache can be thought of as *another* form of politics.

S: But if there is no representation, if the state is not in the middle, then what is the difference between a band of fascists who propose attacking someone and a group of people who are trying to enact justice? What are the criteria in place to say that it's not the same, that there is no parallel between producing an act of justice and just attacking some guy. Specifically, the accusation against the escrache says that because it does not work within democratic politics and the politics of representation the escrache is just a violent attack, and, thus, democratic institutions should take the side of the attacked.

M: This is a critical conversation for us which touches on what it means to be subversive today. There are people who still think in this seventies' mindset: my father, my mother did this or that. . . . And if I want to be at their level I have to go and do the same thing. The experience of the seventies gets boiled down to having guts, to standing up. If this is the case, then, compared to the seventies, everything else comes up short.

This is what people on the street sometimes tell us. There are neighbors who approach us and say, "You just have to kill that guy." And I think this comes from an inability to be able to think of subversion in another manner. It makes it seem like the only form of subversion is to attack someone. We think in a completely different manner; for example, it's more important that the murderer remains silent. The escrache is really an attempt to change, through painstaking work, the functioning of certain social mechanisms.

We don't work in secret, but rather in the light of day. And one thing that is really important for society-at-large to understand is why the escrache has emerged. The escrache has emerged because representative justice has dedicated itself to protecting these murderers. Instead of prosecuting these guys, the police protect them. This is evidence of the fact that, today, there is no justice.

We don't hold on to this resentment, but instead we see these military figures almost as an excuse to work with the neighborhood and to see what we can do to reconstruct our common bonds. It really doesn't matter that much to me if this guy is in jail. We'll celebrate if he does get put in jail, but I doubt that will happen any time soon. The resentment exists, but the escraches transcend it.

Thus, what does it mean to be subversive today? There are tons of practices, which, in the worst sense, are based in a kind of 1970s thinking and which people continue to employ today, instead of trying to rethink this tradition.

It's like when someone says, "Christ, you've got to be kidding me, we're throwing paint at houses and the neighbors are burning the police station?" It's the idea that somehow violence or attacking the state is more radical.

M: What the media and political analysts don't get when they say that the escrache is fascist is that the escrache is not an act of vengeance, but rather it's a process of justice. Which are completely different things. The escrache is constructed with the people, so we do not operate in secret, in the shadows. We are not the chosen ones who have come to take revenge.

M: The comparison has always seemed arbitrary to me. I think it's misleading, because the parallels don't exist in how the escrache is constructed, in its actual methodology. I don't even begin to think about how they are different because I see them as being completely antagonistic.

M: The people who say this don't understand the process that we undertake in the neighborhood. On top of that they're sick in the head.

M: There are people who are just nasty, but there are others who really think this because they're bothered by our refusal to be subordinated to institutions. With the same argument, in spite of the obvious differences, they compared the marches in December to the ones in Chile to overthrow Allende.

M: At the same time, we really don't buy these ideas of "no to violence" or "respect for private property." The question they really want to ask is always the same, "Why do you have to throw these paint bombs?" The other day, for example, we were painting Alacrán's face on a placard in a telephone booth and a neighbor approached us and said, "That's illegal; you can do it on the wall, but not in the phone booth." Incredible; the wall is public space, but watch it with Telecom's phone booth.

M: The escrache is a production of justice and it's obvious that it goes far beyond an act of vengeance. The escrache is a completely different type of protest; it's an invitation to a celebration. It's a celebration where what's destroyed is impotence. There's a power in the escrache that can be accessed by everyone. For that reason, it's joyous, full of laughter, celebration. It's a form of militancy which comes from another place; it's not imposed upon others. When the escrache ends, what you feel is a sense of strength.

M: Moreover we celebrate everything, because we hang tons of posters, because one resident told me such and such a thing, etc. Or this strange thing happens where we go to this guy's house, curse him at the top of our lungs, and ten minutes later we're partying like crazy because we just experienced a moment in which we really felt like there was justice.

M: I remember how when I wasn't in the Mesa the experience of going to an escrache was always different for me from just going to a protest. With the protests you go because you *have* to go, because it's March 24th, etc. In contrast, with the escrache, you feel as if you are a part of the action; it's a completely different experience. For me, from 1983 to the present, this democratic ideology has wreaked a lot of havoc because it hasn't even attempted to reconstruct social bonds. In the neighborhoods, we meet people who come to us and say, "Let's quit fucking around, we've had democracy for 25 years, and we haven't built anything for the future."

M: Even though the escrache does not have a given form, I would never be able to imagine a silent protest, because we try as well to legitimize shouting, singing. In the escrache we are always encouraging each other to sing in order to make the escrache stronger, to identify ourselves.

M: When I was not in the Mesa and I went to the escraches, what happened to me was that I felt like I *could*. There were tons of the things I couldn't do outside of it, but in the escrache I *could*.

7. SELF-AFFIRMATION

S: We also wanted to ask how you feel about the impunity, and the sense of frustration it generates at its exclusion. That is, in one historical moment, the political authority of this country murdered 30,000 people: they could kill your parents but you were not permitted the same freedom. And now, the sons and daughters of the disappeared, their family members, their friends, are excluded from the process of justice.

But what the escrache created was a powerful way to convert this exclusion, this impotence—which inevitably makes you into a subject of lack, a victim—into an *affirmation*, because if you are able to affirm and to not be blocked out by this exclusion, you can turn this resentment into something else, which gives you the chance to become a creator.

In this sense, something happened which is very similar to certain experiences of the piqueteros, wherein a condition of radical, social marginality can evolve—not always and not necessarily—into an unexpected self-affirmation. In this, we can see something common in a number of experiences, which are different from the experiences that we see generated by a "representative" approach.

M: I have thought about how this seventies style subjectivity operates when there are people who continue to think that radicalism has to do with giving up your class identity. Before you had to go to the factory, but now you have to stay unemployed.[27] But to be unemployed is to suffer, and there's no virtue in that. The virtue is in seeing what you can *make* out of it.

---

[27] *Trans.* The word used here, *desocupado*, has a particular meaning in the Argentinean context. *Desocupado*, as opposed to *desempleado*, was a term developed to make a two-fold criticism in discussions of unemployment and has been widely used in Argentina. The first critique the term makes is that of seeing the crisis of unemployment as a social, instead of an individual, problem. Since the term means "unoccupied" instead of "without a job," it inverts the current discourse around employment that views it as a problem of the worker (one must "retool" for whatever the newest economy requires of you). Thus, the term points out that it's not a matter of an individual not having the correct skill-set, but rather a social and political issue. The second critique is directed at the crisis in political representation, as these groups of workers were ignored by both the established unions and by state institutions (see *La representación del movimiento de desocupados en la prensa gráfica: Una mirada* by Cecilia Fernandez and Mariano Zarowsky, Ediciones del Instituto Movilizador de Fondos Cooperativos, 2005).

IF THERE IS NO JUSTICE, THERE IS ESCRACHE: CONCERNING THE DISCUSSION WITH THE MESA DE ESCRACHE POPULAR

colectivo situaciones

1

ACCORDING TO NIETZSCHE, tragedy and nihilism are the dilemmas of modern man, that is to say, the dilemmas of nihilistic man faced with tragedy.

The *nihilist* seeks an ideal, final equilibrium wherein humanity can rest, but in this search he repudiates the present disequilibrium, existence as it is.

The *tragic man* is familiar with this disequilibrium of forces: he assumes that equilibrium is impossible. And he knows, moreover, that existence—ours, everyone's—is lived more intensely if this disequilibrium is recognized as such.

Through nihilism, then, it is possible to understand the tropes of utilitarianism: the world is de-erotized, it is devalued by the fact of not being (still) what we want it to be.

Tragedy—contrary to all predictions—is the capacity to take on *what is* in *all* of its being: the affirmation of the multiplicity of life as pure positivity.

The *sage*, finally, instructs us in that which the nihilist refuses to see; namely, that the *moral*, which separates the good from the bad so as to select only the good and to discard, as the leftovers of existence, the bad, condemns us to denying half of existence. It condemns us to a "juridical" idea of justice. Justice then is judgment: adhesion to the *good*, condemnation of the *bad*. It is necessary to know how to *judge*.

To judge, at the same time, carries out a dual role: on the surface, it condemns or exculpates using whatever means for judging currently prevail, using whatever set of ideals emerges from the accepted—that is, *dominant*—laws and values. This is well known.

But judging plays another role as well and this is the perpetuation of the division that every order must fix in order to endure. Judging, thus, serves to eternalize social and political divisions, via the diffusion of a *moral*.

In a moment during the conversation with the *Mesa de Escrache Popular* one felt the presence of Foucault and his exchange with the Maoists[1] concerning popular justice. It is no accident that Mesa offered Foucault's text as a possible topic for discussion.

The reader that has made it thus far, we suppose, we hope, has read the two dialogues based on the hypotheses proposed by Colectivo Situaciones. In the first encounter, the discussion is with HIJOS and, in the second, with the Mesa de Escrache Popular. We won't try to explain here the differences and continuities between them. We would just note that they seem to us, in a way, to be getting closer, like two rivers that run in parallel but that are converging— not because they empty into the same delta, but because the creeks and streams running between them are multiplying. Which is to say: it is not an ocean that awaits us on some

---

[1]   *Trans.* Please see Foucault, Michel (1980). "On Popular Justice: A Discussion with Maoists." In Gordon, ed. (1980). *Power/ Knowledge: Selected Interviews & Other Writings. 1972–1977.* Pantheon Books, NY.

distant horizon, but rather an inundation from all sides, resulting from excessive affinities.

In the end, perhaps we pushed too hard, but we see in many contemporary experiences—and the Mesa de Escrache is one of them—a renewed predilection for linking ethical action with an element of the *tragic*, which is precisely the link that politics (or at least what until today we've known as such) needs to privately deny in order to exist.

> "Before, when we came to a neighborhood, the first thing we did was to find the plaza and start working alongside the cultural centers and neighborhood groups. This time we came to a plaza that was already occupied by an assembly, a neighborhood in which they were already working: this made us reconsider how the escrache was going to work, why we were going to the neighborhoods. This sent us into a crisis."

> "I would place it in a more pessimistic light, because we didn't know how to work with the assemblies. We don't know."

> "We went to the office of the assembly and we went to the plaza where there was another assembly, but we had practically no dialogue with any of them. It seemed to me like we were going around with blinders on and we couldn't stop to see what was happening. Like we were exterminators that came, worked, and then left. And we thought we just needed to become hegemonic, to add people to our project. Because until then we always came with the new, the novel, and we worked with the neighborhood on something that we knew how to do."

"All of a sudden these people appeared who were doing interesting things and we didn't know how to relate with them."

"We thought: now that there are assemblies, what a year we're going to have! And for nothing. It's really difficult. To begin with, it's very difficult to stop thinking only about one's self, to think that there are other people doing things, people with whom we didn't get along and with whom we couldn't work."

2

THE SLOGAN THAT brings us together is simple: "*If there is no justice, there is escrache.*" Said by those who say it, that is, by those who set in motion the machine of the escrache, it announces: If "there is escrache," it is because there *wasn't* justice.

And, nevertheless, there is a doubling: if the escrache is—as without a doubt it is—an *act* of justice, the slogan takes on a new meaning. No longer is it just a declaration of injustice. It says as well: "If there is no justice, there is *justice*," since the escrache *makes* justice.

Not only, then, does it inform us that there is no justice. In addition, it reveals that there is *something*, an institution apparently that persists in calling itself with this name, but now without content: justice is just judicial *power*. In this way, there is *another* justice.

On the one hand, a legal justice, that doesn't make justice, not even legal.

On the other, a popular machine that produces *acts* of *justice*.

The machine works by reorganizing terms: "institutional justice," "popular justice," "ideal justice," and "when we have the power" versus "real justice," "existing justice, " and "judge and punish."

And from here it self-corrects, expands, and produces its circumstances.

"The escraches unfold justice," "from below," a "justice of *neighbors*" (so it was said after the events of December, during which—and above all thanks to the experience of the assemblies—HIJOS and the Mesa de Escrache returned to using the term justice).

Thus, the *escrache* is being constructed in tandem with the *assembly*.

From the escrache's point of view, the assembly is an ambivalent matter. Copy the escraches of the Mesa? Question their authenticity? Undertake the *generalization* of the escraches? Is it a success or a failure? It's not a question of names, but of the capacity for reinvention. Of the reinvention of time. This is what the Mesa sees in the assembly: the possibility to augment the resistance to time, which reduces everything to a technical exercise, interchangeable, communicable, homogenous, empty.

The escrache is something else: it is "real work," so they say, and it is an action that can't be improved. And they add: to escrache "is not the same thing as to denounce."

As well, to "go" to the neighborhood is not just to pass through. The escrache doesn't just pass by as if it were nothing: it produces a transversal effect. The significance of the escrache depends, then, on its ability to maintain its openness, on not becoming fixed, on not judging, on not devaluing itself or institutionalizing itself—all of which are gestures associated with closing-off, with exhaustion.

The escrache, then, appears as the form that will attempt to evade the sad fate of this epoch swallowing itself and everything that it has produced. However, it is not a radical challenge to existence. The escrache affirms. It affirms even the disaster that produced it. It is itself like one of those wise Nietzscheans who grow wiser precisely because they learn to love a life, which, in order to be (at all), must be lived in tandem with the most horrifying parts of existence.

However, a life affirmed like this, self-affirmed, a life that doesn't believe in fairy tales, in a final solution, or in the fullness of political subjects who seek total justice, this life is able to speak to us of something authentic. It speaks to us starting from existence itself, from perseverance and from an unyielding desire that runs through the city shouting that justice doesn't just *exist*, but that it is produced, and that if there is no justice, there is escrache.

CONTRIBUTORS

COLECTIVO SITUACIONES (WWW.SITUACIONES.ORG) defines itself as a militant research collective. The group emerged from Argentina's radical student milieu in the mid 1990s and has since developed their practice of militant research in conjunction with Argentine and other Latin American social movements. They are the authors of *19 and 20: Notes for a New Insurrection*, also published by Common Notions.

HIJOS (SONS AND DAUGHTERS FOR IDENTITY AND JUSTICE AGAINST FORGETTING AND SILENCE) is a human rights organization created in 1995 to fight against legal impunity granted to members of the Argentinean military dictatorship and to militate for justice for the disappeared.

MESA DE ESCRACHE is a loosely affiliated group of individuals and collectives (including members of HIJOS) who participated in organizing the escraches.

BRIAN WHITENER is an Associate Professor of Romance Languages and Literatures at the University at Buffalo and author of *Crisis Cultures: The Rise of Finance in Mexico and*

Brazil (University of Pittsburgh Press, 2019). Other writing or translation projects include *Face Down* (Timeless Infinite Light, 2016), *De gente común: Arte, política y rebeldía social*, edited with Lorena Méndez and Fernando Fuentes (Universidad Autónoma de la Ciudad de México, 2013) and the translation of *Grupo de Arte Callejero: Thoughts, Actions, Practices* (Common Notions, 2019). He is an editor at Displaced Press and has been investigating new political and artistic movements in Latin American and autonomist political theory for the past twenty years.

DANIEL BORZUTZKY is the author of *The Book of Interfering Bodies* (forthcoming, Nightboat Books), *The Ecstasy of Capitulation* (BlazeVox, 2007) and *Arbitrary Tales* (Triple Press, 2005). His translations from the Spanish include the poetry collections *Song for his Disappeared Love* by Raul Zurita (2010, Action Books) and *Port Trakl* by Jaime Luis Huenún (Action Books, 2008). He lives in Chicago.

FERNANDO FUENTES lives in Mexico City, Mexico and Houston, Texas. He forms part of La Lleca, an artistic, radical education and feminist collective intervention into the Mexico City prison system (www.lalleca.net). He is co-editor of the books *Arte Acción y Performance en América Latina* (2004) and *De gente común: Arte, política y rebeldía social* (2010).

ACKNOWLEDGMENTS

THE TRANSLATORS WOULD like to thank first and foremost the members of Colectivo Situaciones for their commitment to this project and for answering our numerous (hopefully not too numerous) emails and queries. Their engagement has been as priceless as it has been stimulating.

We would also like to thank Juliana Spahr and Jena Osman of ChainLinks for their rich contributions to the original edition and for their comradely permission in offering Common Notions the opportunity to re-place this book in the world. Thanks go as well to Jennifer Flores Sternad, Federico Pous, and Tim Kreiner for their comments and criticisms of the introduction; and to Nate Holdren and the late Sebastian Touza for their trailblazing translations of Situaciones work.

ABOUT
COMMON NOTIONS

Common Notions is a publishing house and programming platform that fosters new formulations of living autonomy. We aim to circulate timely reflections, clear critiques, and inspiring strategies that amplify movements for social justice.

Our publications trace a constellation of critical and visionary meditations on the organization of freedom. By any media necessary, we seek to nourish the imagination and generalize common notions about the creation of other worlds beyond state and capital. Inspired by various traditions of autonomism and liberation—in the US and internationally, historical and emerging from contemporary movements—our publications provide resources for a collective reading of struggles past, present, and to come.

Common Notions regularly collaborates with political collectives, militant authors, radical presses, and maverick designers around the world. Our political and aesthetic pursuits are dreamed and realized with Antumbra Designs.

www.commonnotions.org
info@commonnotions.org

MORE FROM
COMMON NOTIONS

19 and 20: Notes for a New Insurrection
Colectivo Situaciones
With Contributions by Marcello Tarì, Liz
Mason-Deese, Antonio Negri, and Michael
Hardt
Translated by Nate Holdren and Sebastian
Touza

ISBN: 978-1-942173-48-9 (print)
ISBN: 978-1-942173-62-5 (eBook)
$20.00 | 6 x 9 | 288 pages
Subjects: Latin America/Insurrections/
Resistance

**From a rebellion against neoliberalism's miserable failures, notes for a
new insurrection and a new society.**

19 and 20 tells the story of one of the most popular uprisings against neoliberalism: on December 19th and 20th, 2001, amidst a financial crisis
that tanked the economy, ordinary people in Argentina took to the streets
shouting "¡Qué se vayan todos!" (They all must go!) Thousands of people
went to their windows banging pots and pans, neighbors organized themselves into hundreds of popular assemblies, workers took over streets and
factories. In those exhilarating days, government after government fell as
people invented a new economy and a new way of governing themselves.

It was a defining moment of the antiglobalization movement and Colectivo
Situaciones was there, thinking and engaging in the struggle. Their writings during the insurrection have since been passed hand to hand and their
practice of militant research modelled widely as a way of thinking together
in a time of rebellion. Today, as a staggering debt crisis deepens, we see the
embers from that time twenty years ago in the mutual aid initiatives and
new forms of solidarity amidst widespread vulnerability.

Revisiting the forms of counterpower that emerged from the shadow of
neoliberal rule, Colectivo Situaciones reminds us that our potential is collective and ungovernable.

MORE FROM
COMMON NOTIONS

Grupo de Arte Callejero: Thought, Practices, and Actions
Grupo de Arte Callejero
Translated by the Mareada Rosa Translation Collective

ISBN: 978-1-942173-10-6 (print)
ISBN: 978-1-942173-34-2 (eBook)
$22.00 | 6 x 9 | 352 pages
Subjects: Art/Latin America/Social Theory

An indispensable reflection on what was done and what remains to be done in the social fields of art and revolution.

Grupo de Arte Callejero: Thought, Practices, and Actions tells the profound story of social militancy and art in Argentina over the last two decades and propels it forward. For Grupo de Arte Callejero [Group of Street Artists], militancy and art blur together in the anonymous, collective, everyday spaces and rhythms of life. Thought, Practices, and Actions offers an indispensable reflection on what was done and what remains to be done in the social fields of art and revolution.

Every new utopian struggle that emerges must to some extent be organized on the knowledge of its precedents. From this perspective, Grupo de Arte Callejero situates their experience in a network of previous and subsequent practices that based more on popular knowledge than on great theories. Their work does not elaborate a dogma or a model to follow, but humbly expresses their interventions within Latin American autonomous politics as a form of concrete, tangible support so that knowledge can be generalized and politicized by a society in movement.

Without a doubt this will not be the most exhaustive book that can be written on the GAC, nor the most complete, nor the most acute and critical, but it is the one GAC wanted to write for themselves.

BECOME A COMMON NOTIONS
MONTHLY SUSTAINER

These are decisive times ripe with challenges and possibility, heartache, and beautiful inspiration. More than ever, we need timely reflections, clear critiques, and inspiring strategies that can help movements for social justice grow and transform society.

Help us amplify those words, deeds, and dreams that our liberation movements, and our worlds, so urgently need.

Movements are sustained by people like you, whose fugitive words, deeds, and dreams bend against the world of domination and exploitation.

For collective imagination, dedicated practices of love and study, and organized acts of freedom.
By any media necessary.
With your love and support.

Monthly sustainers start at $15.

commonnotions.org/sustain

Printed in the USA
CPSIA information can be obtained
at www.ICGtesting.com
JSHW021549111223
53613JS00006B/102